REMARRIAGE

WHAT MAKES IT · WHAT BREAKS IT

REMARRIAGE

WHAT MAKES IT · WHAT BREAKS IT

HELEN FRANKS

THE BODLEY HEAD
LONDON

British Library Cataloguing in Publication Data

Franks, Helen
Remarriage: what makes it, what breaks it.
1. Remarriage
I. Title
306.8′4   HQ1018
ISBN 0-370-31023-3
ISBN 0-370-31209-0 Pbk

Photoset by Rowland Phototypesetting Ltd
Bury St Edmunds, Suffolk
Printed in Great Britain for
The Bodley Head Ltd,
32 Bedford Square, London WC1B 3EL
by St Edmundsbury Press Ltd
Bury St Edmunds, Suffolk

First published in 1988

ACKNOWLEDGEMENTS

There are many people I would like to thank for helping me with this book. Among them, most prominently, are the people whose names I have changed—those who talked to me of their present and their past, their divorces and remarriages. Also, the following individuals and organisations provided me with their time, resources and expertise, for which I am most grateful: Muriel and Robin Blandford and the Stepfamily Association, Loulou Brown, National Children's Bureau, Christopher Clulow, Family Policy Studies Centre, Dee Knapp, Mavis Maclean, Penny Mansfield, National Marriage Guidance Council, Graham Munn, Renate Olins, Martin Richards, Margaret Robinson, Kay Wellings and the Family Planning Association, Marriage Research Centre.

CONTENTS

INTRODUCTION

This is a book about couples in remarriage, or living in a new partnership after a marriage. It is also about the way people relate to each other during their divorce and in the years that follow, and the effect this has on their children, their present partners and their chosen way of life.

Remarriage is not at all like marriage. It has been described as 'more intricate, less predictable, and far more variegated', peopled as it is with ex-partners and ex-in-laws, children and stepchildren, grandparents and stepgrandparents—so many more protagonists than ever grace a scene when first-time couples marry. But it is still first and foremost a bond between couples who are seeking happiness with each other, and so I set out to explore the quality of remarriage by interviewing couples and individuals about their past and their present experiences, and drawing upon the growing body of research on the subject. I included some people in permanent, committed relationships who were living together with no intention of marrying since this is a choice often made today after divorce.

From this material I began to question certain assumptions and ideas commonly held about divorce and remarriage, the first of which being that when people remarry they choose a new partner who is a replica of the old one, thereby heading for disaster second time around. This is a strongly held belief, often expressed with a degree of know-all hostility. We are making judgements, saying that people who do not learn from their mistakes must take the consequences, and deserve them. This may provide a comforting sense of superiority in those who feel they have avoided such mistakes, but it is not helpful in understanding, or making easier, the process of remarriage.

In over fifty remarriages, I found only one or two where a

man or woman could see similarities between their present and previous partner. People mainly choose—or find—partners who are in fact quite different, if only because they have positively rejected certain qualities once and are aware of not wanting them again.

We see this in women leaving a marriage because they want personal freedom and find they cannot have it with a man who is stuck with traditional ideas about the way wives should behave. Such women are unlikely to choose another man with a similar outlook. We see it in men who leave because they feel they have 'outgrown' their marriages and want a liberated wife rather than someone who is locked into domesticity. We see it in those domesticated wives who look back with bitterness at the years of devotion and support they have put into their marriages and turn gratefully to a new partner who offers stability and appreciation of their loyalty, though he may be less of a high flier, or less passionate and captivating than the partner chosen ten or twenty years ago.

Perhaps most significantly we see it in the way age differences occur in marriage and remarriage. Among divorced women, 37% marry men younger than themselves, compared to only 10% of spinsters. Around 25% of divorced men marry women older than themselves, compared to 10% of bachelors. It is, incidentally, a myth that the majority of men remarry much younger partners. On average, men marry new partners who are about four years younger than their predecessors.

There probably are some psychological repeats even among couples with differences of age or circumstance but they don't have to spell disaster. The second time around, it is possible to be wiser as well as older and to make things work because there has been a change of perception and attitude. When things don't work in a second marriage, it is often because nothing has been learned from the experience of the first. Even when marrying someone totally different, it is possible to remain pretty much the same, with the same insecurities that bring the same demands and quarrels. A woman who is the martyred victim with one kind of man can manoeuvre herself into the same position with another who is quite different. A man who divorces a martyr in favour of an independent woman may find the latter unsettling to his self-esteem in different but equally disturbing ways.

This suggests that some people are divorce-prone, and of course there are those who never learn and remain over-demanding, insensitive or withdrawn, and therefore difficult to live with. But remarriages also fail for other, more diffuse reasons.

The social and economic facts of remarriage provide as much if not more strain than the choice of partner. The legacy of the previous marriage—financial pressures when there are two households to maintain, conflicts over children or stepchildren, tensions and guilts through unresolved difficulties with a for-mer partner, are sufficient in themselves to jeopardise a new relationship. And in the face of these pressures is an attitude that has been defined as 'conditional commitment', the idea that having got out of one unsatisfactory situation, it is possible to get out of another. The person who has been through a divorce acquires different standards of tolerance and forbearance, despite a strong desire to make things work.

Another widely-held assumption about marriage and remar-riage is the importance of communication. In theory, good communication makes a relationship work. Bad communi-cation makes for marriage breakdown. But there's a possibility that communication may be something of an illusion. Women want more of it than men; men think they're getting and giving it in reasonable quantities when their partners think the op-posite. More wives than husbands say that decisions are shared. Presumably, the husbands think they are really making the decisions on their own. But who's right?

Research suggests that neither high nor low levels of com-munication create as much satisfaction in marriage as an *agreed acceptance* of the level, even when it is not very high. Goodwill may be the stuff that oils the wheels of marriage, not com-munication. And it is only when the goodwill goes that the lack of communication becomes a major source of dissatisfaction.

We place too much emphasis on 'high quality' communi-cation in marriage, just as we have in the past placed too much emphasis on high quality sex, thereby creating unnecessary dissatisfaction and unattainable goals.

The most uncomfortable fact about remarriage, when there are children of a previous marriage to take into account, is that it is couple-centred, not child-centred. At a time when children need special support and care, they are witnessing a parent absorbed in making a new relationship work, rather than one who is focusing on them. Women, especially, are torn by their desire to be loving, protective parents and the equally important desire to have a satisfying adult relationship.

Stepparents who come on heavy with the discipline may sometimes be expressing a desire for the children to be neither seen nor heard nor to be present in the flesh, not because they are basically unaccepting or ungenerous, but because they are putting their own needs first. All relationships need time and privacy, especially when they are new. Here is a painful conflict of interests with no easy solution.

At the same time, stepparents want be accepted and to show affection, and may do so to the point of taking over from the biological parent. The term 'sociological parent' has been given to the person (usually the stepfather) who becomes the active parent, especially if the real one conveniently turns up only for birthdays and Christmas and offers little financial support. But children find the whole thing easier if they are allowed to see a stepparent as an addition, not a replacement.

There are two kinds of situation that lend themselves most readily to additions. One is where a financially independent woman chooses a new partner and in no way imposes on him the role of stepfather. This is most likely to happen when the couple live together rather than remarry. Finances are split, the mother supports herself, her ex-husband provides maintenance for the children and everybody is clear about who is involved with whom.

The other positive situation occurs when the divorce is amicable and the ex-couple remain or become friends. When the biological parent is welcomed in the house and is encouraged to keep in contact with the children the conflicts of interest are much reduced.

Unfortunately, the majority of ex-couples are not child-centred in their arrangements. Despite their concern and care, the need to protect children is sometimes overriden by a desire for revenge or feelings of rivalry towards an ex-partner. Anger is extraordinarily long-living after divorce. It is easy to build up on stereotypes of embittered wives and deserting husbands. Ex-partners are seen as a threat to present happiness. They are people to be avoided and resisted.

This brings up another assumption in many people's minds. It is generally considered that there is no such thing as the 'good divorce'. It is merely a cover-up for a couple not being able to 'let go'. This is bad because it not only prevents them from making adequate new relationships, it creates confusion in the minds of the children of the divorce.

In this book, there are examples of several couples who have made positive arrangements after divorce and remarriage. Some of these arrangements are based on compassion, others on sheer practicality. They suggest that life is simpler and much more pleasant for the adults and also for the children concerned, who contrary to received ideas are not confused.

Research into children after divorce shows that they are happiest when maintaining strong contact with both parents. Lesser-known research also suggests that remarriages are happier when there is some positive contact with an ex-partner. Maintaining a state of war is a costly and unproductive business.

Clearly, the values and judgements that we bring to first marriages do not apply to subsequent ones. There has to be an expansion, not a closing in, that embraces both adults and children. We have to discard the expectation that it is normal and natural to hate an ex-partner, and see the feelings as transitional. We deplore the loss of the old extended family, but we have here the opportunity to make new kinds of extended families. At one level, there is the advantage of networking. New marriages bring an enlarged family group. Perhaps an ex-partner who is a teacher can help new stepchildren with their studies. A builder or a dentist in a newly-acquired branch of the family will be able to offer services.

At another level, the new extended families can provide children with an example of tolerance and welcome outside the narrow nuclear group. Non-custodial parents sharing properly in a birthday party, an ex-mother-in-law being welcomed at Christmas—these are just small examples of opening out.

We can be more imaginative about domestic arrangements and the way children are shared, and less condemning towards those who appear to be changing the rules. Only by freeing ourselves from current attitudes can we see new possibilities and explore them without prejudice.

This begins to sound like a plea for remarriage, but that is not the intention. Remarriage after divorce is a fact of modern existence, so we need to treat it creatively. The purpose of this book is to explore the many ways, creative and otherwise, that people do treat it.

HELEN FRANKS, May 1987

Chapter 1
THE SAME OLD STORY

'And then they were remarried, and lived happily ever after' might be the modern ending to any fairy tale. It is, of course, no more accurate than the original version given the high failure rate second time around.

But, for better or worse, remarriage is a growing part of contemporary life. We attend the wedding of a friend or of our children and silently hope it will last or perhaps more cynically give it five years as we are reminded that this is supposed to be 'till death us do part'. We may attend second weddings, more subdued affairs this time, with Dr Johnson's words in mind—'a triumph of hope over experience'. Actually we get it wrong: Johnson was referring to one who remarried hastily, and goes on to say that it is a compliment to a first happy marriage for a man to marry again. The misinterpretation is a reflection of the little faith we have in remarriage, at least among those of us who are the bystanders.

We are of course also the participants. The majority of women (92%) and men (86%) will marry at least once, and one-third of all new marriages are remarriages. About 80% of people divorcing under the age of thirty will remarry within five years. Just over half of women aged under thirty-five at separation will remarry within six years. (For further statistics see page 46.)

Widespread remarriage is by no means a twentieth-century invention. In the eighteenth century, when Dr Johnson made his observation, and for centuries before, remarriage was a commonplace occurrence, not through divorce, but through death of a partner. A listing from the parish of Clayworth in England in 1688 showed that out of seventy-one husbands in the village, twenty-one had been married more than once, and of a similar number of wives, nine had been married more than

1

once. Judging by other records of the times, these remarriages took place with unseemly haste. The idea of promises till death meant something quite different when up to half of those who married in their mid-twenties would not be expected to survive to their sixtieth birthday, as was the case in the seventeenth century. Even in the nineteenth century, only two-thirds of couples could expect to see the wrong side of fifty-five together. No doubt punters at the weddings would privately give their estimate of the chances of survival of bride or groom, while the happy couple optimistically exchanged their vows.

Today, it is not death that casts its shadow over the wedding, but divorce, which is now the major reason for remarriage. People enter marriage with a sense of choice about its future and an awareness that if it doesn't work there is a comparatively easy way out.

There has been a steady rise in the number of divorces in all industrialised countries since 1950. The United States has the unenviable place at the top of the league (with one marriage in two destined to end in divorce), and next come the USSR and Australia. Then there is a cluster led by England and Wales, closely followed by Sweden, Denmark and East Germany. Lowest rates in industrialised societies (apart from no-divorce Ireland) are in West Germany and Japan, though they too keep rising. There are now signs of a levelling out in the United States, possibly due to a fall in teenage marriages, more cohabitation, the caution that may come with troubled economic times, and, of course, the advent of AIDS.

WHY PEOPLE MARRY

In our post-industrial society, couples generally choose their partners for the same reasons as they ever did: for love based on free choice. Letters and diaries quoted by Alan Macfarlane in his book *Marriage and Love in England, 1300–1840*, show that parents had considerably less say than their children in choice of marriage partner. Nevertheless, love and romance were little more than the passport into a new life stage. As John Gillis says in his survey of British marriage from 1600 to the present, *For Better, For Worse*, in the seventeenth century 'love conjured in

2

courtship was exorcised at the time of the wedding. Although husbands and wives were supposed to show consideration and respect, conjugal love was a means to marriage not its end. Too much conjugal affection was perceived as unnatural and a threat to the broader social obligations that came with the establishment of a household.'

Today, such ideas seem unnatural. However, a vestige of it remains in younger and perhaps fairly traditional couples. Penny Mansfield of the Marriage Research Centre followed the progress of sixty-eight married couples under the age of thirty for a period of several years beginning in 1979 and found that marriage was thought of as something that brought social status. It made you into an adult, a person to be taken seriously. The majority in her study lived with their parents before marriage. Many had 'saved up' for their future independence.

Other traditional views emerged when it came to roles of husbands and wives. Women accepted that they would take on the housewife role along with motherhood, and glossed over the fact that even before the arrival of children they were actually doing most of the housework. But their choice of partner was based on more modern expectations, like the idea of equality, the importance of communication—rather more important to the women than to the men—and of course a natural assumption that sex was going to be all right, most of them having tried it out beforehand.

Sexual experience prior to marriage is highly valued nowadays. Perhaps the fear of AIDS will begin to make virginity seem more desirable, but for the present it doesn't rate. If there's sexual compatibility, then that's one less thing to worry about, is the way the thinking goes, making little allowance for the adjustments needed to adapt to familiarity, loss of romance and possible boredom that lie in wait. Penny Mansfield's couples made comments like 'it's better to find out in advance if you are suited. It would be awful to find out on your wedding night,' rather as if sexual inadequacy or inexperience were an incurable, and even contagious disease.

Young people flatter themselves that they are far too sophisticated to marry the wrong sexual partner, which is very understandable. There has been a revolution in attitudes towards sex and marriage within recent living memory. In 1956 *Woman* magazine's agony aunt Evelyn Home could respond confidently to a reader who wrote, with suitably discreet contrition: 'I have created enough trouble for my family already. They forgave me once, and now I am in the same terrible situation again. I have a reckless, impulsive nature and when I am in love, I just can't be sensible . . .'

Evelyn Home left her in no doubt: 'Self pity is not much help in your plight, neither is remorse, unless it is accompanied by a real determination not to sin again.'

Only twenty years ago, in 1966, Aunt Evelyn's correspondents were still caught between guilt and caution: 'My young sister says the best way of loving would be for her to give herself to her fiancé—although he prefers to wait until they marry . . . I have learned through my job as a social worker that sex outside marriage causes more misery than almost any other self-indulgent habit.' Evelyn Home tacitly agrees, reassuring the writer that 'there's not the slightest need to worry as long as her fiancé is not going to accept the gift she's so anxious to offer him.'

But by that time Brook Advisory Centres were giving contraceptive advice to young unmarried girls. Sex before marriage was becoming acceptable, preferably with the fiancé and no one else, and by 1970 the Department of Health and Social Security gave the mandate for Family Planning Association clinics to open their doors to unmarried women. The 1967 Abortion Act reduced the need for men to 'do the right thing'; social welfare improved the lot of unmarried mothers. The morality of Christian and other religions seemed remote and inappropriate, and the sale of brass wedding rings from Woolworths must have plunged overnight.

Along with a claim to sexual gratification came also self-discovery. Feeling accepted and understood counted more than old-fashioned duty and respect, and could be achieved through communication, a spin-off of psychotherapy and counselling, the 'talking treatments'. A *Sunday Times* survey in 1982 revealed that 62% of the sample rated 'being able to talk about your feelings' as the most important ingredient in a happy marriage.

Such aspirations put quite as much strain on marriage as the highly romantic ideals they have superseded, or perhaps even more.

WHY PEOPLE DON'T MARRY

Not everybody stays at home till they can afford to marry. Some leave home long before they are thinking of 'settling down'. For these young people, especially the ones who are lucky enough to have a reasonably paid job, independence comes without marriage. They appear to have it made . . . a climate that allows them sexual freedom, parents who themselves are likely to be influenced by the permissive society, and, especially for women, job opportunities as never before, despite high unemployment.

But the pressures of such freedoms bring special problems to this group. They may be so choosy that they opt out of marriage altogether.

In America, more and more men of marriageable age are living alone – three million in all, nearly 40% of these being under thirty-five. Some of them are likely to be homosexual, a group who in the past might have married in order to deny to themselves and to the world their sexual orientation (and who subsequently might well have helped boost the divorce rate). Women too feel free to choose a lesbian relationship, but many heterosexual women are deferring marriage while they pursue a career. Sometimes, the deferring becomes permanent. Executive women are less ready to compromise than other women according to Leah Hertz, in her book *The Business Amazons*. They do not have the same motivation for marriage as executive males who want a 'caring, listening, cooking wife'. Being financially independent, high-flying women want companionship and an equal sharing of domestic burdens and are not so interested in security-giving, bread-winning husbands.

Cohabitation has increased in recent years in all West European countries, as well as in America (though America showed a slight drop in 1985). In Britain, one out of four couples who marry have lived together beforehand, and increasingly cohabitation is seen as a test for marriage.

5

For the young people represented by these kinds of statistics, the big problem is commitment. Men perhaps fear that women today demand too much of them. The old male-bonding is receding under the critical glare of feminism, and also through the reductions in men-only heavy industry. Women now not only compete for the same jobs as men, they expect men to be active in parenting and more receptive emotionally. Men are beginning to resent the role of sole breadwinner. Women think twice about the joys of family life versus the pleasures and freedom of a career, and are aware of the element of inequality even in modern marriage. Both sexes are conscious of the fragility of marriage, seeing friends and parents part.

Getting together seems often to be a great source of conflict and anxiety for these couples. They may draw up unwieldy contracts about the way finances are to be arranged, whether they should or should not have children, where they should live—near his workplace or hers. If a baby comes along there are more discussions about who should look after it, and maybe at this stage marriage will follow. But not necessarily. Women with earning power may feel they have too much to lose through marriage. Some are prepared to leave a relationship before the baby is born rather than face marital commitment, even those who have to rely on their own parents and social security for support. Freedom of choice can create new and uncharted problems, new kinds of responsibilities that seem very remote from the urge for liberation and permissiveness that set the whole thing in motion.

THE FAMILY CONNECTION

Trashing the family was a great intellectual pastime in the late Sixties to early Seventies. Edmund Leach in the 1967 Reith Lectures told us of its narrow vision, source of all our discontents. A few years later, R. D. Laing and David Cooper were pointing out its oppressive qualities and saying it was bad for our health. Feminists, particularly those in lesbian relationships or with separatist views, exposed the pitfalls for the unwary female. Families were definitely out of fashion.

In the Eighties things are changing. Family therapist Robin

THE SAME OLD STORY

Skynner cleverly called his book *Families and How to Survive Them*, and he had a well-known comedian, John Cleese, to popularise the idea. More significantly, there are hints of a change among the radicals. In a book called *What is to be done about the Family?*, published in 1983, feminists acknowledge that the commune is no more stable than family life, and often a lot less satisfactory. One contributor, Wendy Clark, confesses her need to tell her parents that she is a lesbian. 'The relief was tremendous. Acceptance and recognition from friends and work-mates was nothing in the face of the sense of freedom and exhilaration I had from family recognition.' For of course, they knew better than to show shock or disapproval or rejection. Families may be coming back into fashion but they have lost much of their power and potency. (Indeed, young people with enlightened families have no one to blame for their own wrong choices but themselves. No wonder they fear commitment.)

In right-wing circles, the erosion of family authority is regarded with despair. 'Bring back Victorian values' the cry goes out, disturbingly reminiscent of pleas for the cane or capital punishment. Lack of backbone in the family is somehow held responsible for crime, immorality, violence, child abuse, and any other social ill one might wish to name. And it's all the fault of the permissive society, the women's movement and while we're about it, the Immoral Left. (While some of this might be justified, it takes a right-wing view to put the blame on the home when there is also unemployment, glamorised violence on television and a desire to reduce welfare intervention as part of Conservative policy.)

In actual fact, the disempowered family has early precedents. Before the industrial revolution, when people postponed marriage, and a large minority never married at all, it was common for the poor and the young to leave their families and seek work away from home. In many families, only the oldest son could count on an inheritance of land. Many of the children would go into domestic service, some would drift to towns. As the population rose, crowded cities made immigration attractive. The net result was that the family was neither particularly close-knit nor extended.

In the nineteenth century, at the height of the industrial

revolution, there were changes in the family structure. Marriage became more necessary for women as productivity became factory based and fewer outworkers were needed. Males gaining prosperity enjoyed the luxury of supporting wives and children, who, if possible, would stay home till they were married. Middle-class morality condemned illegitimacy, which was rising almost as quickly as the popularity of marriage. There was a new-found respectability and power vested in the family, which became the centre of morality. As John Gillis points out, the centrality of marriage in people's lives reached a peak which continued right up to the mid-twentieth century.

But the industrial revolution, which did so much to encourage the modern bourgeois family, also helped to undermine it. Gradually it lost its role as producer of basic goods, as provider of education, medical care, even entertainment, so that it became, as it is now, the prime unit of consumption. The size of the family can be controlled, so that child-rearing takes up a smaller proportion of married life, leaving more free time for a couple to explore their own potential and incompatibilities.

Marx was surely correct in seeing industrialisation as corrupting to family bonds, but welfare intervention erodes family responsibility too, and it is an ironic tribute to the success of human inventiveness and compassion that in western societies relationships are no longer needed for survival, but are valued for the personal satisfactions they provide. We are not only post-industrial, consumers rather than producers of goods, but post-Freudian, committed to individualism and emotional fulfilment, and of course demanding a great deal from our personal relationships to provide what American writer Christopher Lasch has called a haven in a heartless world, a defence against bureaucracy and big brotherhood.

In public imagination this is often taken to mean that we do not care for our children or our elderly, we enter marriage and divorce unthinkingly, and we are a thoroughly selfish lot. Statistically, this is not quite true. Eight out of ten severely handicapped children under fifteen and four out of ten severely handicapped adults live with their families, according to a survey from the National Council for Voluntary Organisations. Among women over eighty-five, 38% live with

8

relatives. (Both of these findings are highly likely to depend on the presence of women, the traditional carers within the family.) Most people find marriage break-up difficult and often painful, and 80% of divorcing couples in the NCVO report wanted better counselling services.

Nevertheless, we are extremely active in the breaking and re-making of families. We know there will be pain and problems. We accept that there may be disapproval. But we see ourselves as seekers of happiness. We look to institutions and social services to ease our family burdens. And we don't call that selfishness, we call it a right.

WHY PEOPLE DIVORCE

Alternatives to the single, stable marriage are in no way new. Polygamy was the norm in the majority of non-Western societies, and still is in some developing ones—a convenient set-up when economies are run on female labour and on children, as they are in many parts of Africa. There is a relaxed view of divorce in many tribal societies, particularly where the children are incorporated into the mother's family group.

Until 1857 anyone wanting a divorce in England had to get a special Act of Parliament. Naturally, unofficial divorces took place, though they were not reflected in the divorce rates. John Gillis's book provides many examples of 'wife sales' in the eighteenth and nineteenth centuries. They were slightly less unsavoury than the one conducted by Hardy's Mayor of Caster-bridge, who offered his wife to the highest bidder. More often, there was mutual agreement and a deal was made between the husband and his wife's lover. There were also other ways of getting round divorce, like not marrying in church. Civil weddings, outside the recognition of the church, were undone in a clandestine fashion. Gillis estimates that 'as much as a fifth of the population may . . . have lived in an illicit relationship' in the eighteenth century, and there was much partner-changing in this sector.

It is only since 1969 that divorce has been made really easy, for church and civil marriages alike. Today, there are some changes in who is divorcing and why. Women are seen to be

9

divorce-prone, to some extent because they are increasingly becoming financially independent, but also because some are prepared to risk poverty for freedom from an unsatisfactory marriage. In England, seven out of ten divorce petitions are filed by women, and though in some cases this is through husbands doing what is deemed the gentlemanly thing and allowing their wives to take the initiative, in many it is because the wife has had enough.

Some people may be trying to make up for lost time, regretting the lack of sexual freedom of the past when they were of young marriageable age. The 'menopausal' male having a late fling with a woman much younger than himself is a well known type. But older women are equally capable of late flings, finding themselves free of domestic responsibilities as children grow up, returning to work with renewed enthusiasm and energy, and enjoying, for the first time in years, contact with men as individuals rather than as somebody's wife. This 'adventurous' approach to life plays a major part in contemporary attitudes, and helps weaken the marriage bond. Small families, with children born close together, mean less burden but also less joy and less reward from family life. Fulfilment has to be found from other sources.

Another aspect of this is personal growth—rather more respectable than mere adventure. We value the development of confidence, assertiveness, self-esteem in our pursuit of happiness, though whether those things bring us happiness is hard to say. But it is common for someone seeking divorce to state that 'we grew apart', and we can accept that unconditionally, with easy understanding. And if it is something that seems to be said more often by women than by men, we accept that too, men being traditionally less questioning about their inner development, and more able to take it for granted in a male-dominated society.

Divorce is not the lightweight get-out that moralists deplore. It may invite loneliness, financial insecurity, great heartsearching, especially in women who end the marriage in these circumstances. Even the traditional male way of ending a marriage —through a love affair with a younger woman—is often painful, involving torn loyalties, guilt and regret. Men can feel they have 'outgrown' a relationship too, though their life style is more likely to allow them opportunities to express it by finding another partner. None of this will wash with those who see the pain as far more widespread, affecting the recipient partners and of course the children. 'We are seeing a drying-up of real loving care of children' writes a woman to *The Times*, blaming her own sex for going out to work and thus lending their support to the decline of marriage and the increase in immorality and crime. This loads rather a lot of blame on working mothers, some of whom may be bringing up their children single-handed and with little or no financial support from fathers. Another *Times* writer deplores the idea that it takes courage to walk out of a marriage when 'much greater courage is required to stay and face up to difficulties, honour one's marriage vows and adapt to changing circumstances.'

We cannot turn the clock back to create the uncritical, docile, accepting wife on whom these ideals would depend. If equality between the sexes is an increasing aim among women, then society as a whole, and that includes men, has to find ways to make it work for everybody. It would be an immoral society that could accept anything less.

Not everyone sees a rising divorce rate as a cause for gloom and doom. Some consider that it is an indication of raised standards, a determination to achieve a creative, positive relationship and not be satisfied with a pretence of harmony for appearance's sake. Dr Jack Dominian, director of the Marriage Research Centre said, at the Centre's first conference in 1981, 'Breakdown . . . is a grinding of gears as society moves to a higher level of realisation of human potential through interpersonal relationships. I believe the current wave of divorce is a symptom of the gap between a spontaneous seeking of deeper fulfilment and the lack of education, preparation and support for this achievement.'

It may well be true that we are explorers in an era of intensified interpersonal relationships, and that this is an inevitable part of the progress from a society that survived on labour through agriculture and heavy industry, to a service-and-information-based society, aimed at providing high personal satisfaction, comfortable standards of living and time for leisure activities. With these luxuries within our grasp, we have time to examine and agonise over that we call with self-conscious irony, 'deep meaningful relationships'. We see them worked over and worried at in contemporary literature, film and television, a reflection of our anxieties and fantasies.

Of course we do lack education, preparation and support —or to put it another way, having bought the personal happiness package we need the patching-up kit when things go wrong. But perhaps some people need it more than others. Women have always honed their skill at understanding and responding with sensitivity to their fellow creatures. Indeed, they have had it drummed into them so much that some have rebelled against it, though they are still the ones most likely to turn to counselling for support and insight into relationships. It might be more useful to look to ways of offering specific preparation to men, rather than assuming a unisex approach.

Dr Dominian suggests that marital breakdown is at the centre of social pathology, causing or contributing to such conditions as alcoholism, venereal disease, delinquency, gambling, sexual offences and violence in the family, notwithstanding the fact that these were among us when marital breakdown was considerably less common. Again, there's the unisex assumption, though these are male patterns of behaviour that are being described. Are women really such healers and protectors, when they are so often the victims of such behaviour? And if they flee from marriages because of this, are they to be blamed?

There are some curiously unrealistic attitudes surrounding marriage, from the impractically optimistic sexual expectations of Penny Mansfield's young couples to the idea of finding perfect fulfilment for life from any other typically flawed human being. We may currently blame marriage failure on the women's movement, or the inadequacy of men, and as we do so, more and more people divorce, and remarry, possibly with similar expectations. They take with them the scars of failure, and new pressures to succeed. They create immense tension and torn loyalties in their children, and when they reconstruct their lives, they all too often aim to devalue, if not annihilate, everything that they have left behind.

Some of the people who speak of their remarriages in this

book have tried to explore less destructive ways to deal with their past, aware that for the children it is also the present and future. But few people come properly to terms with a divorced ex-partner. There are many fears, some legitimate, that stop them, and many prejudices too, even though a bitter divorce can sour a remarriage. It may be sad, but it is probably true to say that we need even more education, preparation and support for divorce than we do for marriage itself, and not only for the divorced, but for the remarrieds who replace them.

Chapter 2
UNHAPPY ENDINGS

We may be a divorce-happy society, but when a marriage ends, a great deal of justification, explanation and blaming goes on, none of which quite seems to alleviate the situation. We rarely understand and may not even enquire within ourselves why we married our present partner; we may not fully understand why the marriage has failed, but we tend to make our explanations fit the received wisdom of the times.

The law in Britain offers a number of reasons for 'irretrievable breakdown of marriage'—adultery, unreasonable behaviour, desertion of two years' duration, two years' separation by mutual consent or five years' separation without consent. Since 1984, it is possible to petition for divorce after one year of marriage, and divorce may be undefended and granted on the basis of written statements. About 98% of cases are undefended, with neither party appearing in court.

Women tend to cite 'unreasonable behaviour' as grounds, while men are more likely to cite 'adultery', but not necessarily because more wives are unfaithful. Grounds for divorce may simply reflect what is most acceptable or what is given most importance in the eyes of the person, according to sex or social class. Professional men are most likely to cite adultery, while men in lower social classes cite behaviour.

Divorce is no longer a scandal and not much of a stigma, though it still manages to make headlines when it happens to 'newsworthy' people like royalty, politicians and the clergy who are supposed to display exemplary behaviour. Pop singers and film stars are expected to divorce even more than those who married in their teens, or the unskilled or unemployed—all high risk groups. A survey from *Vem ar det?*, Sweden's *Who's Who?*, shows that among the more eminent, it is those who live irregular, mobile lives who divorce most. That, apparently, takes care of actors and artists, then authors, journalists and athletes, leaving the clergy, farmers' sons and judges at home with their wives and families.

A broader based sample of divorces in 1979 in England and Wales also suggests links with occupation, though in this case it is 'personal service workers' who are most divorce-prone—sales assistants, hairdressers, counter assistants. Members of the armed forces, employers and managers also have high rates, and you have to be a self-employed non-professional or an agricultural worker to have low ones. Job dissatisfaction has been suggested as an explanation for these findings, but the social nature of some of the occupations may have as much to do with it.

Personality may be a contributory factor in divorce according to findings based on a national survey of health and development of people born in one week in 1946, and reported by Kathleen Kiernan. People who show a high level of neuroticism at the age of sixteen are more likely to become divorced eventually than those who don't. People who marry in their teens, come from a broken family, have a low income, have children when young and live in council accommodation are also at high risk of divorce so the statistics show. Perhaps the social conditions account for some of the neuroticism.

Whatever the social causes or the legal reasons used when petitioning for divorce, most people seem to ascribe the failure of their marriage to 'lack of communication' or 'sexual incompatibility', which between them reflect the importance of sexual satisfaction and emotional reward in modern marriage—something far removed from the idea of social responsibility on which marriages in earlier centuries were based.

'My first marriage? Quite honestly I dismiss it. I was eighteen. I left two years later. It was almost a non-marriage. I was brought up very strictly, no sex before marriage, and I married for sex though it didn't work.' *Sue, forty-nine-year-old housewife, married three times.*

'We had a lot of things in common, we were both twenty-two, and he was a fellow student. The marriage lasted about two years, and then I had an affair with my boss. My husband was working away from home during the week, and I strayed, for good reasons. He wasn't that interested in sex. He was a nice man and he would have made a very good husband had it not been for getting married too young.' *Pam, forty-year-old advertising executive, married three times*.

Both these—the teenage and the student marriage—are what have been described by Alvin Toffler, author of *Future Shock*, as 'trial marriage'—no strings, no commitments. In pre-permissive times, marriage, for many young people, was the only way to gain sexual experience. But marriage did, and still does, offer an opportunity to get away from home, to gain stability, or to establish a sexual identity.

For a man, the pressure to have a heterosexual relationship was greater in the Fifties and Sixties than it is today, because of the greater intolerance towards homosexuality. Bob's casual drift into marriage as described here is probably quite common among men, especially those who for whatever reason get through their twenties with little sexual experience.

'I was thirty, my wife was five years younger. We were introduced, got on quite well, and we went out a few times. One day she said, "What sort of a girl would you marry?" I sort of rattled off my ideal woman and she obviously thought she was the woman who was fulfilling that suggested idea. Then one day she said, "My brother is a priest, and he's only going to be around this date or that one, which will suit you best?" I named a date and it all seemed quite jolly really. I was being carried along with a new idea. Before I knew where I was, I was married. If I'd really stopped to think about it properly I should never have married her. As with most men, I was a bit old fashioned then, as I had very strict parents. So all the fun and games of a sexy partner, which she was, was the real promise and attraction, and I didn't stop to think what the long term would be. We had the two children, and I didn't leave till they were five and seven. We were married eleven years and I knew from the start that the situation wasn't ideal.' *Bob, forty-six-year-old architect, married twice*.

Most people do enter marriage with conviction and a hope for permanence. For those who are religious, there may be great problems in coming to terms with the idea that they might have married for sex when they had assumed it was for love.

Norman, now thirty-seven, and a high-powered sales repre-
sentative, was married for the first time at twenty, and remained
in the marriage for fourteen years. His second wife, June,
thirty-five, tells this part of the story:

'He is from a very religious Baptist family, and because of his
religious beliefs, when he felt sexual attraction for her he felt it
must be love. It was crazy, but because of his beliefs, although
the marriage was not working out, he couldn't leave her.'

Perhaps Norman had felt genuine love when he married,
though the idea may be unacceptable to his second wife. If so,
the chances are that he'd feel guilt either way.

Molly, a receptionist in her mid-thirties, had the ultimate of
constraints, being an observing Catholic, but was more clear-
headed about what she was letting herself in for:

'I met my ex-husband when I was twenty. He was my first
boyfriend, and though I was never in love with my husband at
all, it was an earthy relationship at first, a bit sordid really. We
fought to keep the marriage going, for us and for the children,
but it ended after seventeen years. I have had to rationalise my
position in the eyes of God. I made a mistake going into the
marriage, I see that now. But you were compelled to go along
with it after fornication. My husband loved me, there was no
doubting that. At the time I felt guilty because I knew I had
sinned, and so I jumped from guilt to marriage.'

When one partner is unfaithful, he or she may not seek to end
the marriage, but be prepared to keep both relationships going,
much to the frustration of the third party. The deceived partner
may sense something amiss and either force a decision or use the
situation as a way out.

June, Norman's second wife, was first married at twenty and
says: 'It was doomed from the start. I became pregnant and
then miscarried. And it was then that the marriage went astray,
because when I was really ill, my first husband was so uncaring
that I thought, this man cannot possibly love me. I thought,
this is silly, we're not really getting on, so a few months later I
moved out, and then I discovered he was seeing somebody else,
a girl of sixteen who he subsequently married.'

Waiting for the children to grow up before leaving is a
well-known way of handling things, and it often manages to

17

coincide with meeting a new partner when the time seems right, as it did for Ronnie, a fifty-year-old taxi driver now married to Gill, a secretary a few years younger. The couple met seven years ago when Ronnie's sons were seventeen and nineteen.

Ronnie: You can put up with a hell of a lot. I lived with my wife for twenty years and she knew I was cheating with other girls for at least fifteen of them. There was so much lacking in our marriage. But we had two boys and there was no way I was going to leave the boys to be brought up, well dragged up, so I stayed. But Gill can give you the final reasons why we left our previous partners.

Gill: Well, I always said that if ever I met somebody that appealed to me physically, mentally and emotionally, that would be it. My marriage had a tremendous amount lacking. You can carry on, on a level, without any problem whatsoever, as I should imagine a good many couples do, but you know, and only you know behind your own front door what there is lacking, and it's not always sex, money and children. People change over the years, and you realise it probably wasn't the best thing at the time. Or you accepted a lot for the wrong reasons. So a lot is just cowardice or being frightened of being on your own.

Anne, now forty-eight, a teacher, was married to her first husband for twenty-three years, fully aware that she would leave eventually:

'I told my first husband, and I told my children, that I was planning to live alone some years before I left. I had decided not to leave till my children were of age because I felt very strongly that their father was entitled to their company on a daily basis, and they were to his. It is very difficult for people to say in advance without anger that they will leave, and I think that is why people don't do it. You do have to face it yourself before you can do it. I had to accept and face that I could do no more to make my marriage work and that I could not change things.'

HAUNTED RELATIONSHIPS

The ways in which people handle their separation often have far-reaching effects. There may have been disappointment and disillusion going back over several years, a gradual realisation that the relationship has survived on self-deception, and then the anguish of accepting that divorce seems to be the only solution, perhaps using a new relationship as a trigger for separation.

People are capable of horrendously wounding action in their efforts to shore up a marriage. Confrontations and quarrels, intended as an attempt to regain understanding, often serve to alienate and distance instead. Each partner blames the other, failing to recognise his or her own contribution. Eventually silence and withdrawal, with a modicum of play-acting to mislead the children and the neighbours, seem the only mode of existence till the final decision to separate.

In all this, the foundations are being laid for a long, and sometimes very sour, relationship with an ex-partner, especially if children and finances come into it. Amicable separations and divorces do occur, but there is no avoiding the distress of marital breakdown, and whatever happens becomes part of the history of the couple, ready to haunt, or help, a remarriage and the children involved.

Anne left her first husband because she had met someone she wanted to live with, 'which was a sort of unexpected eventuality. When I met him, it became very clear that I couldn't then continue to live with my first husband, and I told him very quickly, a matter of two or three weeks.'

Perhaps Anne needed to meet someone in order to make the leaving easier, and anyway if you are mentally poised for departure, you are obviously vulnerable to the formation of a new relationship. She was a mature student, and the man she met and eventually married was a student on the same course with her. All the same: 'I wouldn't say at all that the reason why my first marriage failed was the entry into my life of my second husband. It was because our marriage hadn't worked *between us*.'

Despite her careful preparation, there was still the inevitable pain. 'My daughter, then seventeen, said, "Oh you said you were going to wait till I was eighteen." And it was a very great shock to my first husband—he was someone who wouldn't face up to things. When you leave someone you are undermining their whole reality and you are tearing down your own life, bit by bit, piece by piece, rather like having a large tapestry which you're unpicking and which you have created. However much you prepare, it is traumatic.'

Having something in common, especially the experience of an unhappy marriage, brings a couple together and is a quick way of establishing intimacy. Being able to share confidences provides an opportunity to explore current unhappinesses and frustrations, and is an outlet for pent-up tensions and unresolved conflicts.

June met Norman, a colleague at work, when her marriage had just broken up, and he, perhaps unconsciously, was looking for a way out of his marriage: 'His wife was just expecting Jeremy, their second child. We were friends and I was telling him about my problems and he was telling me about his. Then he was promoted and travelling all over the country. He said he'd had a vasectomy, because his wife was overweight and couldn't be on the Pill, and I went home and cried and cried, and it suddenly dawned on me that I must think an awful lot more of him than I realised. I told Norman, and we started meeting, and then it was very difficult. There were times when I wrote to him and said I would never see him again.'

Norman did leave the matrimonial home, having experienced much guilt, to the point of contemplating suicide. 'I kept saying, what was I doing to everyone, to the children, to my ex-wife, and to June? But then I decided I was the person making the decision. I was no longer going to be prepared to accept that I was going to bury my feelings. I let them rise to the surface, and I said I can't carry on. At which stage, I moved out. My ex-wife never asked me to stay. Never. I don't think I would have stayed, but if there was any feeling on her part, surely she would have struggled to keep something, but there was nothing at all, no fighting.'

Would it have helped if Norman's wife had put up a fight? It might have served further to justify his leaving, and therefore reduce the guilt, or it even might have made him reverse his decision. The fact that the issue is brought up now, five years after the separation, suggests a great deal of unfinished business, which shows in the present circumstances, as will be seen later. The need to create blame, or concentrate on it rather than seeking ways to alleviate it, seems to be a major part of the baggage that's taken into a subsequent marriage. Lack of fight doesn't have to mean lack of feeling. To a wife presented with the final blow, there may seem nothing left to fight for, or the risks of a fight may be too great, as Chrissie's story shows.

Chrissie, now thirty-nine and happily remarried, recalls the break-up of her first marriage:

'We were passionately in love, and very close. We had the same interests, same tastes, same sense of humour. My friends used to say, we're so jealous of you, you're so lucky. We were married eight years and there were two children. Then his father died and I felt after a few weeks he wasn't coping. I can remember suddenly feeling very depressed by his distance from me, and I suddenly asked, is there someone else? and he said yes. The world just crumbled to my feet. It was as if someone had turned the light out. It was a typical situation, a secretary in his office who had just got divorced. I spent two weeks red and swollen-eyed, and he walked about like a zombie. He said he wanted me still but wanted to get away.'

At this stage Chrissie did not fight. They were living abroad —Chrissie's first husband was in international banking—and she decided to return to England with the children. 'I don't know whether that was right or wrong, but of course the temptation was too much and he stayed with the woman. Finally he did come over, and I said I must come back, I must fight for the marriage, and he said if you do, I won't be there.'

So of course Chrissie stayed in England, to build a new life for herself and her children.

Steven, now forty-four, and an engineer, recalls his first wife's fight to reclaim him and his attempt to do the 'decent thing':

'I'd gone to live with Sandra, my present wife, and then I went back after a few days because there were these histrionics. I looked at my first wife and thought that she was likely to do something really stupid. Looking back now I think a lot of it was probably put on, hysterical behaviour designed to get me back. I don't think she would have jumped under a bus or thrown herself over a bridge, but who knows? I'm not at all religious, but I think that if you get married you take on a responsibility which you do your utmost to uphold. I stayed for nine months and then I left, firstly because I realised that I should not have gone back, and secondly because she was driving me out, waking me up in the night as soon as I fell asleep and shouting "you bastard" and thumping me. And the fact of the matter is that she has never forgiven me.'

Another fact is that ten years later, Steven hasn't really forgiven himself. 'I didn't have a bad marriage. I wouldn't say it was a brilliant marriage, and I feel the guilt quite a lot, so I can't blame the poor girl for going to pieces. Having said that, I think she should have learned to live with it and look forward to what matters for the children and her new relationship—she remarried quite soon after. But she hasn't. I've searched my mind a great deal over the years and the older I get the more I blame her for the way things have gone between us, the bits and pieces that have disturbed my relationship and have disturbed hers. Sandra has found it very difficult to forgive me for going back, and I don't think she ever will completely. But I really destroyed somebody's life there, at least temporarily, didn't I?'

The answer one is inclined to give is, hardly, seeing that Steven's ex-wife's present husband moved in within two or three weeks. But guilt can be very enduring, not only because of the sensitivity of those who feel it, but because of the compulsion of those who inflict it.

Sandra, Steven's second wife, recalls those difficult early days: 'Steven went back to see whether he could make a go of it. I suppose he had to do it his way. I was very hurt and let down, and he knows how I feel even now.'

Her own marriage had ended after twelve unhappy years, and she had left knowing Steven was not free to be with her. 'It did not break up because of Steven, but he was the galvanising force.'

Sandra was fifteen when she met her first husband, and the marriage was dominated by her contracting what appeared to be a vaginal infection. 'He called me unclean, and I believed him. We could never grow together as a young couple because our sex life had so many problems. We were always very careful and used a sheath, and I was always getting treatments and ointments to put on.'

After nine years of marriage, Sandra had a brief affair with another man. 'I told him about the infection and he said he didn't care. And then nothing happened. There was no infection. I can only think that somehow I was allergic to something in my husband or it was psychosomatic.'

Three years later, Sandra met Steven and decided to leave her first husband. 'There was a terrible row. He said that I was leaving to be with Steven; although I was involved, it wasn't the real reason for me. But I think it may have helped my husband to survive in some way. It was something to hook onto.'

It may well be easier to blame a third person in order to avoid looking into the weaknesses and difficulties of the marriage. Blame and anger directed towards any single person is often suspect and deserves further examination. Life is rarely that simple.

Bob's marriage breakdown was considerably more laid back than Sandra's or Steven's. 'My ex-wife knew this man who was really a friend of her sister's. He'd been kicked out of his own marriage, and he asked if he could stay in our house and pay rent for a short while. I said yes, and then I was off away working for some weeks, and I guess they got pretty friendly. He is a carbon copy of her, he would cut the lawn, do the washing up. And she said, look, I'm much happier with Phil, I want you to go. And I did. I'd actually just met Sylvia for the second time, though we had known each other for about a year—we are married now—and when I moved out of the family home I moved in with her.'

All this sounds highly convenient, and that's exactly what it was. Phil made the perfect substitute husband when he himself was homeless. Bob was perhaps relieved to find decisions being made for him, just as they had been when he first got married. Both the women were happy with what they were getting. It all seems quite civilised. And yet it also seems too easy. One hopes there was some feeling, some regret, some sealing of the past and recognition of its worth. Would Bob's children, as witnesses to the event, have welcomed such a lack of intensity between the couple who gave birth to them? A decent ending demands at least some tears with which to honour the past.

Not everyone has the convenience or solace of a new partnership when a marriage ends. Molly, struggling out of her Catholic marriage, felt increasingly alienated from her husband. 'We were living comfortably, both earning well, and had a terrific social life. But we had terrible fights and he knew I was wanting to leave. OK, I got sexual gratification, but an hour later at a dinner party I was cringing, because this wasn't my man. Then I withdrew as far as intimacy was concerned, and he became very aggressive. But finally he saw there was nothing more between us and he left. Looking back, I see that I was sustained by my family. I have a tremendously interesting family, a very humorous family, lots of fun. My brothers and sisters are very close. In the right relationship I would have been inclined to veer off. I don't need the backup of my family, but I certainly used them to the full at that time.'

The large family, welcoming with open arms, is a comparative rarity today, but even if it weren't, the tradition of going back to mother seems out of place for some women, when they are trying to break out of a traditional mould. Instead, they are likely to become more independent.

Janet was set up to be the typical company wife. Married at twenty-two, with three children under the age of five, she was living abroad with her oil company executive husband. 'It was the ex-pat atmosphere. Big fancy houses with nothing to do but plan the next big dinner party to keep yourself occupied. I couldn't tolerate it, living a second-hand existence. It was not what we had planned. I had supported my husband through his studies, and never thought he would want to lead that sort of life.'

The couple became more and more estranged, with Janet, as she now sees it, 'nagging and demanding and that made him withdraw, while I had the comfort of the children, and I suspect that was very excluding. I really like my ex-husband, and I couldn't bear to see him so diminished by the circumstances. He knew that sexually we weren't getting on and it ended up being very destructive between us.'

The family returned to England on company leave, and Janet said she would stay on with the children. It was, in fact, the end of the marriage, with Janet's husband returning to his job abroad to complete his contract.

'My eldest child was about to start school. We sold the family house and made a lot of money on it. And he was totally honourable about the money side. We agreed to go on being parents. I wouldn't have left if I hadn't had complete trust in him on that score.'

Harriet, now thirty-seven, was in a very good position to achieve more independence when she ended her marriage, which she did amicably yet with cold efficiency.

'I think a lot of marriages go wrong when children arrive. We were blissfully happy for seven or eight years before our son was born. I had given up my career prospects and worked from home (as a computer programmer) right through to the birth. While I was in hospital after my son was born, my husband was concentrating on his work, and it suddenly dawned on me that I didn't need this. He was concentrating on his work and he wasn't giving me anything that I couldn't do for myself. Then we tried to have another child to patch things up and I discovered that he'd got a girlfriend. I was two months pregnant, he was just beginning to be successful, and he was removing his love from my household to somebody else's. So I immediately took action, had a termination and chucked him out forthwith. I was taking terribly decisive action because this person was not serving any function in my household. He was not earning all the money, because I was earning a good salary. I think the fact that I was independent made it much easier for me, though I must also say that it was a terrible shock. It's a reflection on the choice you made in the first place, and a reflection on your ability to co-exist with somebody. I immediately started proceedings, to get it over with. I think I was able to talk to him reasonably and be good friends really because I took the initiative and didn't feel the downtrodden female with a baby and no job.'

IS DIVORCE BAD FOR YOUR HEALTH?

Divorce is supposed to create stress and even disaster according to various pundits. Social psychologist Michael Argyle has suggested that marital breakdown increases chances of suicide, imprisonment, heart disease, road accidents, with men affected significantly more than women. Men are thought to be left without support during divorce, with no one to confide in, no close male friendships to fall back on (which may well be one reason why more men remarry than women—to find company, someone they can trust, which many men can do only with the opposite sex).

Women don't get out of it lightly either. They may find themselves much the poorer, isolated from the company of adults, burdened with children, and somewhat unwanted socially in circles where the couple rules supreme, and a spare woman is seen as a threat to wives.

Children are in the most vulnerable position of all, possibly taking on some guilt, perceiving the break-up as their fault, or simply hoping for the improbable, i.e. that their parents will reunite. And while they are having to make mental and physical adjustments to a new way of life, they may find that their parents are too preoccupied to help them. The famous long-term study of children in divorce, *Surviving the Break-up*, by Judith Wallerstein and Joan Berlin, shows that the main disturbance to children at the time of divorce is through parents' inability to give love and support because they are angry and depressed. Older children may find one parent leaning heavily on them for solace and sheer company, thus receiving an extra burden of split loyalties and responsibility.

It must also be said that separation and divorce can bring a tremendous sense of liberation, an end to tension, friction and indecision, and possibly a radical change of outlook in the adults concerned. A study from Strathclyde University in 1983, called *The Politics of Separation and Divorce*, suggests that divorced people, women especially, are more politically conscious and concerned about economic reform than married people. An advertising agency, Wasey Campbell-Ewald, coined the word 'divorcynic' after commissioning a report on the attitudes of the divorced in 1982. They found that their respondents were tougher-minded, more cynical about advertising and marketing ploys and less susceptible to sugary clichés than married people. Women especially wished to be addressed in advertisements not as helpless victims but as people with choices.

This is beginning to sound rather more healthy. 'Life events', of which divorce can be counted as a pretty big one, may be periods of growth, times of reassessment, once the initial crisis has been lived through. Helen Weingarten, of the University of Michigan, interviewed first married, divorced and then remarried men and women, and found that the divorced were less likely to report feeling happy than the other groups, but more likely to mention personal strength as a quality they felt they possessed. They were just as likely as the others to assess themselves as having self-esteem and being in good health.

In the divorce/remarriage jargon, there are expressions to describe those who want the divorce—*initiators*—and those who have to accept it—*recipients*. A report, *Grounds for Divorce in England and Wales*, published in 1986, showed that when husbands are the initiators, they are more likely to remarry than their wives, and when wives are the initiators, they are more likely to remarry than their husbands. This suggests that initiators may have a replacement in mind, and are likely to be in better shape emotionally than recipients.

The truth may be somewhat different. Obviously, the person who leaves a marriage because he or she has found a new partner will not suffer from loneliness and is less likely to be financially deprived and bitterly resentful than the partner left behind. And the woman (it is more commonly the woman) who leaves for personal independence may also be happy with the situation.

But the person who appears to be the initiator of the divorce may be less in charge of events than meets the eye. Christopher Clulow of the Institute of Marital Studies has identified a group that illustrates this point: 'We see a pattern in which for quite a period of time a woman has been feeling dissatisfied and the husband has been unaware or turning a blind eye. It would appear as if the man has more control over the relationship, may be better educated or better endowed in certain respects, but then the woman makes this break which she may have been thinking about for years and it's as though the man has been hit by a bolt from the blue, quite unprepared but fighting, and fighting helpless. So he goes next day to the courts to initiate proceedings. He becomes the initiator even though he is the rejected party.'

Fighting helpless often includes turning to the courts on child-related issues in order to recover a sense of influence and control, according to Clulow, though this may become less of an issue once resignation settles in. Remarriage may quickly follow, as a fast way of dealing with the loss and finding a substitute. None of this, naturally, would endear the ex-wife or enhance the couple's future dealings with one another.

Clulow has been working with a team at the Institute following thirty families found through a Divorce Court Welfare sample at Richmond, Surrey. He sees the man who quickly seeks a substitute as one who 'doesn't want to grow and wants to recreate the kind of climate that existed beforehand, restoring the *status quo*.'

Len, aged sixty, is somewhat typical of this. His first marriage ended at his wife's request after eighteen years. 'I still don't really know why. I thought we got on very well, and the three boys have all turned out well. But she said she wanted the marriage to end, not for anybody else but because she wanted to be on her own. I knew it was true. She'd let herself get very fat and unattractive. I'd always been faithful, and I felt bitter about it in the end. I started going to a divorced and separated club, and the second time I went I met Jean, my present wife. Well, I wanted to get married again, and I did within two years. She's a good-looking woman, ten years younger than me.'

Now this marriage is ending, after eight years, and Len blames the failure on the presence in the home of Jean's troublesome teenage son. 'But she says it's not that. She moved to a separate bedroom two years ago. She said she didn't want to sleep with me anymore.' Perhaps whatever Len didn't learn from the failure of his first marriage he still hasn't learned, but in any case he feels he is finished with marriage, though not with women. 'Love them and leave them,' he says, hoping to reverse his previous history and perhaps lose his dependence on the opposite sex.

Pam, who left her student husband, remarried very quickly, and within two years was wanting a second divorce. Unlike

Len, she was undoubtedly the initiator, but was equally confused, though she found a different way to deal with her
emotions.

'I was in my mid-twenties at the time, and my second
husband, who was also my boss, was a man nineteen years older
than me. He left a wife and two children for me. I didn't feel
guilty at the time because you don't behave rationally when
you're in love. But gradually I found this man I had married
extremely square. He was a bit set in his ways, and I began to
pull away from him, especially sexually. I began not to want
him to touch me. I felt my life was in a complete mess and I
decided I'd have to go. It was absolutely ghastly. I decided I
must have therapy. I felt there was something wrong with me,
something I couldn't blame on the outside world. I started what
turned out to be nine years of therapy. I think I went to
someone good, but you never know what it would have been
like if you hadn't had it. All I know is that I thought I was
unmarriageable, and now, at forty, I have been happily married
to someone for five years.'

Perhaps women are more prepared than men to examine their
failed relationships, since they are expected to, and do, give
greater weight to emotional matters. When they leave after a
long marriage, and after much heartsearching, as no doubt
Len's first wife did, they are often prepared to go through a
period of reassessment, enjoying a sense of separateness and
autonomy, according to Clulow. But it can still be swings and
roundabouts for a woman with young children and little earning
power and the problems of being alone in a couple-orientated
world.

Janet, who left her ex-pat life with three young children in
her care, saw herself pouring all her energy into her children,
and then out of desperation and loneliness launched into what
she calls a 'disastrous affair which made me realise that I needed
help . . . so then I went to a therapist for two or three years, a
woman who helped me immensely. I was earning very little
money working part-time for a publisher, and she charged a
nominal amount. I mention that because sometimes people
read this sort of thing in books and think oh god another middle
class wanker with pots of money. But it was very important. It

really helped me to get straight. I saw how close I had come to making my husband feel irrelevant and incompetent. He was feeling a write-off as far as I was concerned, and that was very demeaning for him. But I also knew that he should never have accepted a job abroad when I had said I didn't want that, and at a time when I was suffering from post natal depression. I realised that I never wanted to be identified as the Wife again, on whom these sorts of choices would be laid. I just don't ever want to be someone else's property. Even if he himself did not think of me like that, the world does. I was told by his colleagues and their wives that if we didn't go, his career would suffer, and when I finally said yes his boss said, "I thought she'd see reason".'

This kind of reassessment is one of the best things that can come out of a divorce. 'It has helped in my relationship with my ex-husband, and I think it helped the children too,' says Janet, now in a stable partnership of four years' duration.

Margie and Graham broke all the rules about mourning and allowing themselves space before they made a new relationship. They met through a divorced and separated club within a month or so of being separated, and married a few months later. Both in their early forties, and married now for six years, they had previously been in settled marriages for fifteen and fourteen years respectively, when Margie's husband suddenly announced that he was moving out to live with someone else and Graham's wife said she was having an affair and didn't want to live with him anymore.

For Margie, with a handicapped son who was then fourteen, and three younger children of between five and thirteen, it was a terrible blow. And for Graham, too, it was a disastrous time. His job collapsed, and he decided to emigrate to Canada. Margie agreed to accompany him, with the three younger children on a visitors' ticket, keeping on her council house. They had known each other for a few weeks but did not feel committed. It was something to fill the gap. Says Graham, 'I used to say that there was never anything more that I could think of to do than seeing her again. It was very much day by day.'

Canada did not prove a success. Margie hated it and

returned. Graham soon followed, found another job within a couple of months, and the couple married.

They reacted to their personal losses in very different ways that are fairly typical of the different approaches men and women may take.

Says Margie: 'I did my grieving and mourning while I was married to Graham, which was rather sad. It took a long time. I would say a good four or five years. I drank heavily, took the proverbial valium and that kind of thing to blot out feelings. I grieved not for the person so much as what we'd had. I missed a lot of silly things like laughter and fun. Graham is a very serious person. I was used to somebody who chatted day in and day out . . . Graham's marriage hadn't been good and you'd thought about leaving anyway when the children grew up, hadn't you? She actually told you she was having an affair and you stayed on for three months. You did your grieving bit there.'

Graham is not sure. 'Well, not exactly. I haven't mourned. When my ex-wife told me about the affair I could have killed her on the spot and I regret it to this day. I could have done it in passing rage. People get away with it all the time. So I went through a lot of emotions. I suppose I did my grieving at work because I had nothing to do but sit around all day with the job having collapsed. So I put my energies into finding somewhere to live. I was shocked. It was an awful shock.'

At this point Margie recalls that the affair, so he had told her, was common knowledge. 'Everybody knew except you . . .' And Graham responds stereotypically: 'It turned out afterwards. I was preoccupied at the time.'

Like many men in an unhappy situation, he had thrown himself into his work, spent much time away from home, and was as distanced from his sons, then eight and eleven, as he was from his wife.

Having broken all the rules and suffered many of the consequences, Margie and Graham have survived. 'We decided to jump in with both feet,' says he. 'I'm a bit like that anyway,' says she.

Not everyone can throw themselves into something new. Chrissie, returning to England with her two children when her husband said he didn't want her anymore, went through a period of mourning after what she had seen as an idyllic marriage. 'For a long time I never lost hope, then a friend took me out and was absolutely brutal, telling me to get on with my life and stop hoping. But I had to go through with the mourning. I never really hated him, I was just wounded to the quick. But I could have killed her, the one he went off with. If I'd had a bread knife I could have rammed it into her.'

Where do they go, these murderous feelings? They lie dormant, under control most of the time, possibly unfinished business forever.

Chrissie expressed some of her emotions by having an affair. 'It was an old friend, and much too soon. I'm sure that I made use of him unwittingly. I needed it to have it proved to me that I was lovable because I felt that there must be something horrible, disgusting about me—too small tits or something—and that's why my husband had stopped loving me.'

This is typical female over-investment in physical attributes as a means to lovability, though not so illogical given Len's comments above. Women as well as men need to prove themselves at times through their sexuality, though men tend to make conquest the proof of their lovability while women use approval as the test.

Renate Olins of the London Marriage Guidance Council has referred to 'desperate cruising' in both men and women seeking affairs and new partners after divorce. 'But what is so dreadful about being on your own? If people could stay with that a while to experience how dreadful or how undreadful it really is, they wouldn't feel so driven into rushing into something new. From a counselling point of view, the help needed is not necessarily how to do better in a next relationship, but how to live better with yourself.'

Words of counsel indeed, but sometimes a spell of desperate cruising may be part of the cure (though it also rebounds when other wives sense the situation and close off social channels, especially when they also sense their husbands wanting to take advantage). Both Janet's and Chrissie's desperate affairs may have contributed to that building of personal strength and self-esteem that Helen Weingarten's research showed. The important thing about a desperate affair is that it shouldn't turn into a desperate permanent relationship, or a desperate way of life, and is best with someone who can recognise the terms and is preferably unattached. The period of separation and divorce is an extremely unstable one, a transition that may need professional help. Not everyone can afford or want private psychotherapy, but marriage guidance counselling provides a less costly and more widely available alternative. There are more details about who helps in chapter 10.

THAT'S THE WAY THE MONEY GOES

'Technically, of course, we merely did the modern thing: we split everything down the middle. Everything, that is, except what could be the single most lucrative asset of our marriage —his newly earned post-professional degree. I'd put him through school, yet he would keep an earning power that had doubled while my own stood still.' The quote is from an article in the American magazine *MS* by Marianne Takas.

By way of contrast, here's more of Len's story. 'I sold the family house when my first marriage ended and we split the profits. I did not continue to support my wife as there was some insurance that was due, and she had that, but I did continue to support my younger sons and she asked to borrow £5000 which I lent her and have never got back. My wife had had a part-time secretarial job and then went back to work full-time. She is now well-paid and has been promoted. I have always worked free-lance (as a draughtsman) and have no job security. Now I am about to sell my flat and my present wife wants half the profit. I hope she will only get a third. She has a good job and has contributed nothing to the flat. It seems to me extremely unfair that I should come off so badly when I didn't want either marriage to end.'

There are many divorce stories revealing injustices to men, which is why the law was changed in favour of a 'clean break' rather than the 'meal ticket for life' arrangement. In fact, the Matrimonial and Family Proceedings Act 1984 has not, in many cases, left women destitute. Short-term maintenance orders are very common, though they can be reviewed after three years and the amount paid may be reduced if the courts find altered circumstances. A revised arrangement could mean a final lump sum and no more maintenance payments.

Mavis Maclean, senior research officer at the Centre for Socio-Legal Studies in Oxford, claims that the 'alimony drone' syndrome is a myth, but so is the totally irresponsible father in the majority of cases. 'We surveyed 300 families for up to ten years after divorce and found that the vast majority of men who have an income do pay something, however small. It may not even be registered in the court, and could be only a fiver a week—for a woman a bit like having some extra family allowance. The most common reason for not paying is unemployment.'

The research showed that the majority of young people getting divorced have few assets—'Even if they had bought a flat there may be nothing there when a marriage breaks up after five or seven years. When there are no children, the husband is likely to stay in the flat because he pays the mortgage, and the wife may get a couple of hundred pounds.' When there are children, they usually stay in the family home with their mother. This can often turn out to mean a financial strain, since the home often has to be run on a reduced income.

Mavis Maclean's findings come from observation of young working-class couples. In the book *Divorce Matters*, Martin Richards suggests that overall 80% of maintenance orders are seriously in arrears or unpaid, and that at any time there are about 2000 men in prison for non-payment. This is not mainly because they won't pay but because they can't.

When they can, there may still not be enough to support two households in the way to which they have been accustomed. Alex Goldie, of the Cranfield Institute of Technology, questioned seventy-two predominantly middle-class men aged thirty-five to sixty-five on their maintenance problems, and found that the unending nature of maintenance payments to ex-spouses was a cause of bitter resentment, especially when the ex-spouses were thought to be capable of supporting themselves and were living in the former matrimonial home with another man. Appeals under the new Matrimonial Act brought relief in some cases. It was noticeable that the men did not object to paying mainten-ance for their children, and one man who won a substantial reduction of payment to an ex-spouse, which was offset by an increase to his child, still expressed satisfaction at the outcome.

Despite many fathers' attempts at some kind of maintenance, the usual result is to leave the unit of mother and children decidedly impoverished. Marriage during teens and unemployment are two factors with a high divorce risk, and both mean that the ex-husband is not in a position to provide financial support. Nor, inevitably, is the wife. Kathleen Kiernan's study of teenage marriage and marital breakdown in a population group followed up over a period of thirty-two years, showed that 80% of teenage brides left school at fifteen and by the age of twenty-six only 23% had any kind of job qualifications.

It has been calculated that a mother and two children require 75–80% of the former family income in order to retain a standard of living enjoyed before separation. Since most of the former family income is likely to have been earned by the man, there is little chance of the average one-parent family headed by a woman having or even eventually attaining that original standard.

American research from Stanford University shows that at one year after divorce, a husband improves his standard of living by an average of 42%, while the wife's income drops by 73%. The author of the work, sociology professor Lenore Weitzman, blames the no-fault divorce laws, which are similar to those in Britain. In America, these tend to result in the fifty-fifty split, which means the man retains half the value of the property, and the woman, with children, retains the other half. To achieve the split, the family house is sold, leaving the father with more income and earning potential as well as capital to spend solely on his own requirements. Professor Weitzman recommends that child-support should be decided on an income-sharing basis, pensions and retirement benefits should be viewed as marital property as should the career potential of the husband.

Mavis Maclean did not find such extreme changes in living standards in Britain, but has no doubt that childhood in a one-parent family means increased poverty. She sees the main problem as stemming from women's earnings being so much lower than men's, which means that the only way out of the poverty trap for many women is remarriage. Of course, this is a happy solution for many people, men as well as women, but not everyone will desire it or achieve it, and the underlying assumption that women must be dependent materially on others for their survival is unsatisfactory to say the least.

All the interviews in this book involve people who are remarried or cohabiting. For some, the financial problems are long over, for others they remain bitter reminders or current sources of friction.

Harriet, who had an abortion and ended her marriage when she discovered her husband was having an affair, feels that her present good relations with her ex-husband spring from the financial arrangements. 'I made a deal with him. I said I'd keep everything we had at the time, and that would be it. There was the house, and the car and the furniture we'd bought together. I took over the mortgage, which was about £13,000. That may sound daunting, but he has a very good salary, and he'd just got an excellent job after all the years I'd helped him. He does pay half the cost of our son's maintenance, but that causes him no problems. Our arrangement means that it doesn't ruin any future relations he has, so that if he wants to remarry there will be no financial problems.'

Running the ex-matrimonial home alone is not a strain for Harriet, as she has a well-paid job and also takes in a lodger. Unlike the American woman quoted at the start of this section, she does not feel cheated of her husband's earning potential, and is not concerned about the inherent inequality that implies. By taking 'everything' she leaves him free to use his future earnings as he likes.

Norman and June are more typical: 'When I left I took nothing,' says Norman, echoing what most leavers say. Of course they take nothing, since it is extremely difficult to sort out furniture removal when one is at the height of desperation or sneaking out in fear or guilt. Only the very ruthless, who will clear a house when the partner is away, or the very reasonable, who will plan and negotiate in advance, can take more than the minimum with them.

Norman's ex-wife is also more typical than Harriet. With two children, then five and seven, and no job, she will have needed 'everything' that Norman left her, plus maintenance for herself and the children. June, Norman's present wife, recalls: 'When we got married I had a good income, and she got two-thirds of my salary. She didn't have to go to work.'

When the couple married three years ago, Norman went to the bank and got a second mortgage on the basis of his salary compared with his likely maintenance payments. 'When we bought this place we budgeted on both salaries, but June was basically working to keep my former wife and children. We were able to buy the house because June had some capital, having sold her own property. When we knew she was pregnant we made an application to solicitors about reducing mainten-ance, but were told that we would have to sell this house and buy a smaller one. We had to prove that June's equity had helped purchase the property and I couldn't afford to pay out as much as I had before. We managed to get it reduced so I no longer pay my ex-wife maintenance, but I had to deny interest in the former matrimonial property, though it was in joint names, and I was offered £5000 to lose interest in the house.'

This does not sound at all unreasonable, but Norman and June are angry.

Norman: 'The next thing we hear is that she is getting married again. If I'd known that when I had an interest in the property, I could have insisted on my proper share, which would have been something like £15,000.'

June: 'They're buying a new car and things for the house. It's apparent there's plenty of money to go round.'

And so it goes on, with distrust and rancour given every opportunity to flourish.

There is rancour for Ronnie, too, but with two earners and only one dependent child in the two marriages, there are fewer tensions. Ronnie, now fifty, had a small mortgage to pay off after twenty-two years of marriage. A taxi-driver, he was looking forward to easing-up and working a three-day week. But his divorce totally changed his financial situation. 'My sons are in their twenties, and support themselves. I found I had no claim on the family house though it was in joint names, because I put my name to the deeds of Gill's house when I was buying her ex-husband's share. I had to raise a mortgage to buy the house and he wanted it all sorted out. At the same time I had to pay off the mortgage of my former house, which was just £1,600, as a deal instead of paying maintenance. Altogether, I got a settlement of £3,000 out of a house worth £70,000 which I put a lot of work into. I had to pay legal costs and outstanding debts out of the £3,000, and all I got in the end was £500. Meanwhile, she is living in the house with her boyfriend. Not that I care. I don't wish her too much harm. I'm very happy.'

For Gill, the arrangement leaves her better off. 'Ronnie earns more than my ex-husband did, but of course he has to pay a bigger mortgage and this house isn't worth as much as his former house. My ex-husband does not support me financially, because he doesn't have much money, but he supports emotionally where our son is concerned.'

The fewer dependents there are, the more amicable the arrangements, because financial arrangements are less complicated. Anne, the teacher who left her husband after many years of forewarning, had this aspect planned too. 'We had a country cottage, so I lived there and my former husband kept the town house. I was studying for a degree, and was able to do so from the cottage. My children spend their holidays in the country, as they had always done. I tried extremely hard not to disturb anything. I think what made the divorce amicable was the fact that we did not go to court, we did not consult solicitors and I did not demand maintenance. My priorities were the relationships, and I knew from talking to people and reading that the minute you start getting involved with lawyers, who are doing their best for their client, you start trying to get a better deal and that can mean destroying relationships. I was not prepared to do that, though I knew I was financially disadvantaged as there was a vast price difference between the cottage and the house.'

Anne was living in the cottage with a fellow student, who became her second husband. 'We were both on student grants —he is twenty years my junior—and when we finished we tried to find jobs. We did anything, and lived on social security when we had to. My first husband was a fairly well-off businessman, so this was all very different. I don't think I realised how poor I was till one day I went to see my bank manager and he said, are you destitute? and I thought well, I suppose I am, though I did have a roof over my head.'

Many women, feminist or not, would see this as feeble. It is certainly unfashionable. Perhaps the only criterion appropriate is based on motive. To put up no resistance to unfair claims, or to make no claims out of weakness can lead later to resentment and recrimination, or even to self-blame. But Anne seems to have made a carefully measured decision, thought out well in advance. She acts from personal strength.

Chrissie blames herself for bad handling of money. 'A very thorny subject. I wasn't ready to cope with it and I was wet and weedy and moping and weeping. My father badgered me to get the money sorted out, and wrote me long, boring letters with everything carefully listed. So eventually we did get it sorted in that money was coming regularly from the States where my husband was still living. He was earning a socking great salary. I didn't like to ask him for money, I felt sad asking for it. I don't know why.'

Too unromantic perhaps? Too much of an acknowledgement that the marriage had really ended? Or simply a case of a woman being too nice, equating a standing up for rights with being aggressive or greedy or even unladylike?

After a few months the couple agreed to get a divorce. 'As he was away, it was all done through lawyers, and really fairly amicable. The fact that I didn't understand a word when my lawyer told me what I was signing may have helped. I had to be led by the hand and hoped that she was doing the best for me. I took along a friend on one occasion who is extremely capable and practical, and she said later she didn't understand a single word the woman had said either. She talked in such jargon. One of the things she said was that my ex-husband did not have much capital and the best thing was for me to accept mainten- ance for myself for only three years and then only maintenance for the children because she was sure that by then I would be remarried. So I said yes, thinking that seemed fine, but in retrospect I'm not sure that was really a good decision. As it happened, I was married again within four years. But I did have the house, and there was only a small mortgage to pay off.'

Clearly, there is no guarantee that a woman lawyer will offer a woman client a progressive solution. Many will view women the way men do, and the way women have been brought up to do, which is as people who are viable if marriageable, and who base their future on that potential. As long as women do not earn equally and remain the sole nurturing parent, they will look to marriage for their salvation.

This created sense of dependence in women inevitably becomes a burden for men, though they resolutely hold on to the role of main breadwinner. Some, out of a sense of guilt or to avoid hostility, will be extremely generous to an ex-wife, especially if there is a hint of blackmail about access to the children. Ian, a teacher aged forty-five, willingly gave up his claim to the flat and to a country cottage, and even the family car when he divorced. 'I knew I'd have to start from scratch, but I didn't mind. Friends said I was soft, but she had earned more than me, and the cottage was a legacy from her parents, and there were the children. I didn't want to lose them, and I didn't want to be on bad terms with their mother.'

Even the ex-husband who can financially afford a dependent, 'alimony drone' of a wife, may feel the burden in other ways. Gerald, a property developer in his forties, is easily able to support his ex-wife without causing hardship in his second marriage. 'She is quite wealthy in her own right. She has a house of her own, several investments, and a property in Portugal. I did not want to reduce her standard of living and I am fully supporting her financially on top of this, though she could support herself from her private income. But she is clinging, she won't let go. She bought her house two miles away, as close as possible. She is on her own with a succession of short-lived and unhappy affairs. She is depressive, losing weight, has a very poor relationship with our teenage daughter. A casualty, I'm afraid. One of the ethics of my family is that you look after the women, but I'm beginning to feel that she should be making a move towards independence and I should give her less financially. We are encouraging her to get a job for her self-respect and to make her more self-sufficient, but she is resisting. We've had all sorts of things thrown at us by the family, like suppose she commits suicide, and we say this is what we genuinely believe is better for her. Letting her stay reliant upon us isn't helping her to grow up. And of course it isn't helping us either. We have been visiting a family therapist, and have tried to get her to come with us but she does not want to get through her grieving.'

So money does not always solve the problem, and may intensify dependency. Unhappy ex-wives who 'take their husbands to the cleaners' may not be greedy or dishonest. They might be fearful, insecure, needing to cling and asserting a last-ditch bid to restore normality with the little remaining power they have. Similarly, not every ex-husband is deliberately selfish and withholding, but again might be acting out of desperation. But people when angry or humiliated can be incredibly vengeful, and short-term self-interest often gets in the way of long-term satisfaction, not only for the ex-couple, but for any new permanent partnership that might follow. Unhappy endings can create a legacy that casts a blight on happy beginnings.

Chapter 3
BEGIN AGAIN

'No more second marriages. One punishment is enough.' The sentiment was expressed by a 'screamer', one of those distressed beings who shriek out personal woes on public highways. Heartfelt as it might be, most people view the situation differently. Of marriages in 1984 35% were remarriages for one or both partners. Of those divorcing under the age of thirty 80% will remarry within five years.

Alvin Toffler's predictions in *Future Shock*, written in 1970, seem nearer and nearer to reality. We are witnessing young couples entering into what Toffler called 'trial marriage', with a decision made in their early twenties on whether there will or will not be children. (Such couples today may well buy a property together, but cohabit instead of marry.) This is followed by a marriage that does include parenthood, and if by the late thirties that doesn't work, Toffler predicts a third try in a partnership between 'two mature people, presumably with well-matched interests and complementary psychological needs'. Even then the experiment isn't over. There's the idea of a possible 'crisis point' at retirement, and yet another 'punishment' on the horizon. Perhaps the self-imposed restrictions on sexual adventures through risk of AIDS will reverse these trends.

Despite the familiarity of remarriage, those who look at it from the outside are not terribly comfortable with reminders of its existence. People register when there is a great age disparity in a couple, and do a quick sum about her age and the age of his oldest child. Those who pre-empt curiosity by saying this is my second marriage, invite even more conjecture. We like to hang labels on people, and the remarriage label has certain connotations and something of a stigma . . . divorce, failed relationship, other woman, deserting husband, secondhand rose, wicked stepmother.

Second weddings tend to have a rather subdued quality compared to firsts, as if it is bad taste to celebrate too enthusiastically. Letitia Baldrige, author of the revised *Amy Vanderbilt Complete Book of Etiquette*, is quoted in *New York* magazine as saying that a second marriage ceremony should be a 'quiet and private affair—only for the couple's family and closest friends,' though the reception can be 'as big as you wish'. Even the present-giving is of a more modest nature, which may be expected if parents have gone through it all in a big way once and feel that their offspring are or should be more self-supporting this second time. And the presence of family from a previous marriage may call for a certain delicacy—Baldrige says it's O K to have stepchildren at the ceremony ('a lovely way to welcome the children into the couple's new life'), but goes into a faint at the thought of wedding guests who are ex-spouses, ex-lovers and even ex-in-laws, otherwise known as grandparents, unless the ex is deceased. All this illustrates a certain narrowness and nervousness about the whole business. Despite the unreality of pure, first-time virginal love, it blends more easily with the traditional white wedding, even in its contemporary flawed form.

Religious ceremonies are not a common part of second weddings, though in recent years there has actually been an increase in remarriages of the divorced solemnised in the Anglican Church. A 1981 resolution from the General Synod of the Church of England gave the custom approval under certain circumstances. A vicar may marry a divorced person in church, irrespective of his bishop's views. In England and Wales, about 14% of divorced men and 10% of divorced women remarry with a religious ceremony. Americans appear to be more at ease about this, with the comparative figure at 62% and 60% respectively. Religious remarriages in the Roman Catholic Church remain at a steady 5% to 6% in England and Wales, permissable when annulments have been granted. There are in fact increasing numbers of applications for annulments.

John Haskey of the Office of Population Censuses and Surveys suggests that the greater preference for religious ceremony by men reflects those marrying spinsters or widows, who may desire the ceremony more than a divorcee marrying a bachelor or widower. This presumes either that more divorced women than men have abandoned the Church or that couples base the suitability of a religious setting on the bride's putative virginity. Or, of course, both.

Feeling disqualified from a religious ceremony can cause genuine deprivation that can have an effect on the relationship according to Audrey Baker, tutor with the National Marriage Guidance Council. 'There are those who never feel properly married because their second marriage could not take place in their Church—and this may increase a sense of guilt and failure and cast a blight on the new relationship.' On the other hand, pure pragmatism can relax strict rules about intermarriage. Among Jewish circles, where high value is placed upon family life, parents who would not condone marriage outside their own religion for their children will do so more readily for the divorced of their own generation.

One might ask in these liberated times, why—with the exception of those with religious conviction—remarry at all, why not simply set up home together? Many couples do cohabit, at least for a while, but many also say that there is pressure from family and friends to remarry, though this may be a convenient disguise for their own wish to do so. We are a society that is addicted to marriage as the 'correct' and therefore most secure life style, and most of us do want security and some promise of permanence and continuity. Living together in some people's eyes doesn't have the 'feel' of permanence.

Even worse than cohabiting is the man or woman living alone. It is no wonder that friends and relations want to see the unmarried settled. They are less of a psychological problem, a social liability, a threat to existing marriages or even a pertinent reminder that there is a satisfying existence to be had either partnerless or without a marriage certificate. Remarriage may generate a sense of unease but it is more acceptable to the married community than divorce or single parenthood.

Jacqueline Burgoyne and David Clark, in their study of forty remarried couples (*Making a Go of It*) say: 'Without remarriage the family life of the divorced does not attain full societal legitimacy,' a reflection that applies alike to the attitudes of friends, relations and protagonists, though the latter are most affected. It is assumed today that people worry less about conforming and that, for instance, a career woman is unlikely to care about marriage and security. But this is not universally true, and many still retain a need for 'respectability'.

June was adamant that she would not live with Norman before marriage when he left his first wife, though she was over thirty, divorced, with a home of her own and a well-paid executive job. 'I'd lived with someone before and I couldn't get along with it. It just wasn't me and I felt awful doing it. I didn't feel right not being married. I suppose I'm very old-fashioned . . . it was uncomfortable with neighbours and it was awful when you got things through the post. The neighbours obviously assumed you were married and I had to explain that I wasn't.'

Burgoyne and Clark found similar embarrassments over names in their couples when cohabiting. There seems to be a need for what is considered normality, or at least appearances of it, in some circles. So much depends on who the neighbours are—and the majority are still married couples.

But there is more than appearances at stake. Says June, part-time stepmother to Norman's children: 'The church that we go to . . . last week somebody came up to me and said, Oh you've got three children now, haven't you? And I said, No, only this one is ours, Norman has two from a previous marriage. And I hated doing that, having to admit that he, well, had that behind him . . . I don't mind people taking me for their mother, but I mind when they ask and I have to say . . . I have to be honest, but that really hurts me, really upsets me.'

Ironically, 'normality' in contemporary society often means appearing to have a fairly laid-back, casual view of previous partnerships and the passions that might have accompanied them, but June's morality is of a more traditional nature and she is voicing a gut reaction that is rarely acknowledged. Stepchildren, financial tangles, the presence of an ex-partner of flesh and blood, the memory of a deceased husband or wife who can no longer make mistakes, create a past that impinges on the present. The effort to play the part of average young marrieds, with evocations of the ideal couple, true love forever, busily building their nest, is constantly sabotaged.

45

Remarrieds, whether widowed or divorced, have a history that refuses to fit with romantic and religious concepts of one flesh and a spiritual union that endures on earth and in heaven. There are many ways in which they cope and compensate, from moving to a new geographical location to rejecting the ex-partner. Divorce and remarriage are as lucrative for estate agents and household manufacturers as they are for lawyers.

AGE AND EXPERIENCE

Contrary to popular belief, not all divorced men remarry women much younger than themselves. On average, second partners are about four years younger than their predecessors, according to most recent findings from the Divorce Reform Association. About 90% of men marry a woman younger than themselves in their first marriage, as against only 75% in their second. (Men normally in first marriages not only marry women who are younger than they are, but women who are less educated and of lower work status.) When both partners of a remarriage are divorced, they are likely to choose someone of fairly equal age.

Divorced women are also more flexible about age in remarriage, with 37% marrying men younger than themselves compared to 10% the first time. This is a dramatic switch. It may mean that divorced women find younger men more open and responsive than older men who may have very traditional ideas of what a wife should be. Children are no bar to a woman finding a second husband, but age is: only 28% of wives aged fifty or over at divorce remarry, compared to 47% of men. Widows are less likely to remarry than divorced women.

Several of the women interviewed for this book were either married to or living with men much younger than themselves. Here are some who illustrate various problems and non-problems.

Sue, now forty-nine, has been married to Jim for thirteen years and they have two children. He is ten years younger than she is. Both have been married before, Sue twice. Neither are remotely bothered by the age difference.

Says Sue, 'He was twenty-six at the time, I was ten years

older, but we had both been through marriage and divorce, and we both had children before. Age didn't come into it, except for other people gossiping.'

Anne, aged forty-eight and remarried six years ago to a man twenty years her junior feels similarly. 'On the whole, I didn't have people round me who would raise their eyebrows. There are people who will judge by appearances, and people love to gossip on very little evidence. I met with a fair bit of hostility from relations and friends. My daughter is only a year younger than my second husband, but the children have been wonderful. My only sadness was that I had a miscarriage at forty-two. It was a devastating blow for us.'

The doubts and heartsearchings are forgotten as the reality of the relationship provides its own reassurance and the sense of commitment increases, but if you have to keep away from gossips, they obviously have an effect. You don't want to hear your own doubts voiced by those you feel are hostile. You may not want to hear them from those you trust either. Remarrieds with a big age difference must feel a sense of isolation and implied criticism, however temporary, which may serve to bring them closer though not necessarily encourage them to be more frank about the issue.

Harriet has been living for four years with a man fourteen years her junior. She is thirty-seven, he twenty-three and a student.

'I am very conscious of this. All sorts of problems arise. Well, the idea of having children comes up in flashing lights. I wouldn't mind having another child, but it would have to be soon, and it isn't fair to ask a twenty-three-year-old to make up his mind once and for all now. We are very attached to each other. Virtually remarried. There is no problem living together, but there might be a slight problem where status in the household is concerned . . . He is earning a third of what I am earning, and it's my house. I think it would be more satisfactory if we lived in a house we owned together, and I hope that he will eventually buy a country cottage so that will be his house.'

Harriet is the first to see that such issues are not issues at all when it's the man who is older and owns the property. 'Because then the man is looking after you. But we got together soon after my marriage broke up, and he looked after me wonderfully then. For about six months he was quite ready to comfort me at regular intervals without getting fed up with it. So the problem of who is head of the household doesn't matter very much because I feel he is looking after me.'

These are somewhat surprising words from a woman who earlier expressed pride in her independence. The convention for men to marry women slightly younger than themselves probably evolved out of the superiority of male earning power, certainly not out of who matures first or who lives longer. An older, and therefore wealthier, man would be more desirable to some women, who would appreciate his extra maturity, too. What this also meant was that men were able to bestow protection and paternalism upon 'their' women in return for housekeeping, bearing children and supplying the emotional background of family life, a state of affairs many women today find highly unsatisfactory. Harriet's is an example of a new kind of relationship in which each person contributes what he or she can, regardless of traditional roles.

The more common set-up of older man/younger woman may have modern complications. Pam, whose second marriage when she was in her twenties was to a man nineteen years her senior, felt pressure on her to have children, though her husband had three from his previous marriage. But the thought of the future because of the age difference made her fear the idea, and contributed to the marriage failing. 'I was a young career woman and very ambivalent about having children anyway. His former wife was very domesticated. I think he was very happy with me, but our age difference at a time when young women were wanting more independence than traditional wives was part of the rift between us.'

HOW DIFFERENT THIS TIME?

Remarriage is not only about restoring normality, it is also about correcting mistakes, showing the world that this time everything is going to be all right. There is a general belief that people remarry someone very similar to their first partner, but remarrieds generally profess the opposite—they need to demonstrate to themselves and everyone else that choice number one was an error of judgement, therefore choice number two has to appear to be very different.

There are exceptions to this, of course, and often they are the ones that don't work. A recurring choice of partner who is a reflection of an unsatisfactory parent may signify an inability to be mature and at peace with the self. But remarrying a similar person can mean making a better go of it the second time.

Anna and Bruce really did marry the same people again. They first married when they were aged twenty, were divorced when they were twenty-six, and remarried each other four years later. They are now thirty-four, have a young baby and their first home of their own.

The couple met on holiday in Greece. Anna returned to her native Sweden but then decided to join Bruce in England. She gave up her studies to do so. Bruce at the time had left school with no A levels and had poor job prospects.

Says Anna, 'We weren't going to get married. We were having dinner with Bruce's father and he said why don't you two get married, and we said all right. It just happened to us, really because his parents found it hard to accept that we should just live together.

'I don't really know where it went wrong. We were too young. We hadn't done anything on our own. I started work in a secretarial job that I didn't want to do, simply to pay the rent. I felt a bit trapped, I'd made the sacrifice and left my country, and also I couldn't study, I couldn't have the life I'd had before. Life changed so drastically. I was so used to Scandinavian freedom and independence. That simply disappeared. I had expected that my husband would be as liberated and would contribute as much to the home as I did.'

There were other strains on the marriage. Being a stranger to London, Anna leaned heavily on her young husband, who was as unfamiliar with big city life as she was. 'I expected Bruce to know how things worked, and he didn't. I'd never been dependent before, and I resented it. I felt, why doesn't he understand how to find a job, or a flat. I was dependent on someone who couldn't be depended on for no fault of his own.'

49

To add further complications, Bruce decided to go back to studying to qualify as a civil engineer. He met new people, widened his social horizons and had a brief affair. Anna couldn't accept it. 'I felt, you either commit yourself to someone or you don't.' She also resumed her studies and arranged for a divorce. When Bruce qualified, he decided to work abroad, and the couple parted.

But they never lost touch. Says Anna, 'We telephoned. We wrote. I visited his parents.' Says Bruce, 'Seeking each other out when we separated was something we both wanted to do. A natural gravitation rather than a conscious decision. It's easy to say now in retrospect that we found that we were each other's best friend, even when we were apart. We could discuss things with each other better than we could with anyone else.'

Both Anna and Bruce see the coming-together as gradual and tentative. 'We got to a point when we said, "Let's carry on" . . . It wasn't easy to face the fact that we had made a mistake to part. Although it was awful, in another perverse way it was healthy. It was a kind of cure, and cures can be drastic,' says Bruce.

He is not quite sure how and why things are different this time. 'It is facetious to say, Oh I'm the one who's changed. Really, it is imperceptible. I used to say, Oh you nag too much. What I see in both of us is more of—to use the current word—*glasnost*. Because I think we were living in a terrible cocoon, wanting to hold on to that one person all the time. We weren't part of a world out there and that was stifling for both of us.'

Anna is more decisive. 'What is different this time? We talk much better. We don't quarrel about what happened in the past. I can verbalise it whereas it makes Bruce very unhappy to think about it, though he is able to talk about it now. I'm prepared to give more, not so intransigent as I used to be. I didn't marry the wrong person, I married at the wrong time. Now I am the homemaker, but it is a choice I've made. I think it has maturity behind it, not just compromise but an active choice.'

The only false note in this happy reunion is the weight of guilt still felt by Bruce. 'I still do have certain nightmares about blame, blaming myself. I'm sometimes conscious of the idea

—does she trust me . . . I do trust myself 100%. It's like the man who does not want to go into a police identity parade because he's afraid he'll be picked. He knows he's innocent but somehow fears he will be blamed.'

Perhaps there is still an element of blaming inside Anna which needs to be acknowledged. All the mistakes of young marriage, a woman from a different culture, a man still finding himself, a mutual over-dependence contributed as much to the failure of the marriage as Bruce's brief adventure. They did marry the right person, but at the wrong time, and that's a lot to ask of any marriage.

When a remarriage choice is a deliberate move away from the original, it may be related to the new image a person has of him or herself. After his drift into what he sees as a suburban marriage, Bob felt that his social circle had been too narrow, and this was why he had married the wrong person. 'What happens is that people marry within a very close group. They happen to go to a party and meet someone who lives near. If only people would go far enough afield and stretch their horizons, they would be in a better position to pick the right partner. You need to experience an enormous number of people in order to say yes, that's the sort of person I should spend my life with.'

A vision of a world cruise comes to mind, a sort of global consumer test. There is a popular view that experience at a spatial level provides wisdom—and it's true that teenage marriages fail because couples haven't had time to meet many people or to know what they really want in the long term. But you can't sample that many relationships, and it is only by experiencing one in a fairly deep way that you really learn anything from it, as the previous couple, Anna and Bruce, found.

In fact, Bob met his second wife, Sylvia, because they had office accommodation in the same building. Sylvia, in her mid-thirties and twelve years younger than her husband, has not been married before. She has an independent working life, running her own import business.

'I knew immediately that she was what I needed. She is a woman with a career, unlike my first wife. I wasn't stretched before. I am now, to the limit. We both have independent lives

51

because of our jobs. We travel a lot, separately, for instance. My life style has not changed but I am now married to someone who understands and lives the same way herself. We share doing things around the house, but I did a lot before because my first wife was a very untidy person and I've always been fussy about cleanliness and tidiness. And thank goodness, my second wife is fussy too.'

Being compatible very much includes having similar standards of hygiene and tidiness, though few people think about such things before marriage. Oddly enough, it was men who talked more about this, while women seemed to be more concerned with character difference and the form that quarrels take.

Steven and Sandra, both forty-four and married ten years, see each other as very different from their previous partners, and feel that they have changed each other because of that.

Steven: I was absolutely horrendous about the house and my ex-wife was a real untidy bitch. But Sandra is much more organised, and it changed me a million per cent. Nobody changes entirely, but what changes is the pattern of your life. Before I met Sandra I was a pretty bad lad. I mean, I used to go out all over the place. Selfish, terribly selfish, I'd come in late at night, drinking. I wouldn't dream of doing anything like that now. I'll even come home early rather than stay out with colleagues after work for a drink when I know we're just going to have a quiet evening watching television.

Sandra: Our rows are quite different. We blow the roof off mainly because I shout back now. I used to find it difficult to get angry. I thought something awful would happen. I'd destroy who I was angry with. I don't feel that any more. We do have awful rows, but I'm sure they spring from more passionate feelings.

These must be very typical stories. Unhappy husbands stay out, get drunk, neglect their wives and their children. Unhappy wives lose interest in the home, fear they will get out of control if they voice their protest, and indeed often do. In a survey of 335 divorced and separated men and women on 'Perceived causes of marriage breakdown and conditions of life', both men and women listed 'lack of husband's time at home' as an issue, along, of course, with lack of communication and sexual incompatibility.

Many, exhausted by 'temperament', choose a second partner for compassion rather than excitement, as Harriet has done.

'My ex-husband is an extremely entertaining man. You know, it is terribly difficult being married to somebody like that because you have heard all the jokes. Everyone who meets him says what a marvellous man, and it is difficult when you divorce because your parents can't see what can be wrong. But these marvellous entertainers are not so marvellous at home. My ex-husband used to drink too much, smoke a lot. He wasn't terribly self-disciplined. Unlike a lot of people who go for a carbon-copy of their ex-husband, I've gone for somebody who is completely the opposite. He is quiet and gentle, someone I can trust.'

Margie and Graham, who met and married very quickly after their previous marriages ended, may have weathered their storms together because whatever faults they have found in each other, they can also contrast with faults in the previous relationship. Graham's cold first marriage was very different to the warm, noisy family life he shares with Margie and her children. 'I don't feel worried, because she tells me how she feels,' he says, which must have helped him through the bad times when Margie raged and mourned. And though Margie may at times miss the fun she had with her outgoing first husband, she also remembers his violent temper. 'I put up with a lot of verbal cruelty, a lot of smashing of things in the home. He's very rigid. Graham is so laid back and easy. I am totally relaxed with him. But I must say that anything could happen in the house and he wouldn't be aware of it. He has a low response to emergencies.' To which Graham replies: 'It's deliberate because we've had so many emergencies—the roof fell in, we got flooded, there were Margie's operations (hysterectomy, gall bladder) and her breakdown. If I'd responded to them all I'd be worn out. I try very hard to go for stability as the most important thing.'

So it's swings and roundabouts. When Graham's first wife raged and mourned over her failing marriage, she must have done so inwardly, turning against a naturally reserved man who emotionally turned his back on her too. It is not something Graham can do with Margie, precisely because she is more demanding. And though she now has a man who is less of an extrovert, he is not one who will get up one morning and say he is leaving, as her first husband did.

Chrissie, aged thirty-nine and remarried to Mark aged forty-three, also switched from a charismatic partner to someone less extrovert, after her idyllic-seeming first marriage ended equally abruptly, 'He is so different. I met him in the office. He was divorced, rather shy. We had a lot of interesting things to talk about, one of them being divorce. He has the same interests as I shared with my first husband—complete and utter enjoyment of music. But he is strong and mature, whereas my first husband is like a little boy. We never quarrelled, though I would harangue him. With Mark, we can have a good argybargy. He is obstinate and will stand up for what he thinks, and I admire him for it. Now, instead of trying to keep things buttoned up I do tend to say when I feel resentment or anger, perhaps because he is less tempestuous and I am more of an extrovert than he is.'

One thing Chrissie is aware of is that though her second husband is different, there are some ways in which nothing has changed. 'I don't think I myself am very different as a person with Mark. I can see myself falling into the same ways, which is what I didn't want to do. I had lost my independence in my first marriage, and because Mark is so good to me and wants to look after me I can see myself relying on him a lot, and I feel that's not a good thing, though he enjoys having someone to care for.'

This is hardly surprising. We may choose a warm partner after a cold one, a stable partner after an erratic one, an imaginative partner after an unimaginative one, and behave differently in the relationship in many ways. But we are still ourselves with our old insecurities and, possibly, some acquired habits of relationship which are hard to outgrow. If a new partner is happy with them, there is no incentive, and sometimes no good reason to outgrow them. But the differences that we perceive in a new partner may be something of a cover-up, and deep down we might still be seeking the same things as we always wanted and may even have temporarily acquired when we chose our first partner.

It can be difficult to come to grips with the fact that a second partnership, though happy, actually lacks certain things that were present in an earlier, failed marriage. And inevitably, the more relationships experienced, the more opportunity there is for comparison.

Sue, married, for the third time, to Jim, has had several passionate relationships. Her first marriage, at eighteen, was brief and unimportant to her. The second, to a gifted but often depressive man, Nick, was complex, with strong bonds and shared feelings long after it ended. Then there was a turbulent relationship lasting several years with Don before her marriage to Jim whom she chose because 'He gave me peace of mind, something I'd never had.'

Jim, who married for the first time at seventeen to a girl a few months younger, just a year after his mother died, finds in Sue a mixture of vivacity and good nature, and enjoys the stability he brings to her life and to her son from her second marriage. 'We don't row. It's not in my nature to row, though I did in my first marriage. Nick (Sue's second husband) wasn't happy to see his son in an environment with adults fighting, which was happening all the time when Sue was living with Don.'

All this is well appreciated by Sue, but 'Sometimes I wish we did more, not that I want rows, but I feel that if there is something that really upsets me my only way of dealing with it is to "out" it. Communication is the one area where we don't work well. I try to change it because Nick and I could talk about things for hours and hours. Don and I wouldn't talk, but it would come out in a fiery flaming row—and this is why Jim thinks it's wrong. Because things are said in a very distorted way. He's probably right. But there was communication. With Jim, it comes to a point where I'm doing it all on my own, pouring it out to a silent person who is likely just to go out. This can so frustrate me. There are times when this lovely peace and warmth is driving me insane. I've told you this Jim, haven't I?'

Jim nods. They are both using the interview to call a truce. Often that's the best that anyone can do.

Janet, aged forty, and living with her present partner since four years ago, sees a mixture of good and bad differences when comparing her present relationship with her past marriage. 'My boyfriend—what else can I call him?—is much more emotional, and more overtly childish than my husband, who was an academic, very intellectual and clever. He is very creative, a designer and he has been very encouraging about me making a change towards creative writing. This is very important to me. My husband, well, he didn't actually deride, but academics do slightly pooh-pooh people. He would only read the finest novels and the finest poetry, so for me to be a scribbler meant that my aims would obviously be set very low.'

Living with somebody creative does make for difficulties, Janet finds. 'Sometimes he wants someone to talk at, about what he's up to, and I want the same, and we're both quite selfishly concerned and find the other person lacking in sympathy because there's not enough energy there to be promoting yourself and to be caring about the other person too. But that's the price you pay for having a lot of freedom, a lot more space of your own to do your own thing. And there are so many things we can share. He can understand about the dead days, and I can give him a working method because I am a lot more disciplined than him. My husband did not make these demands of me. His work side was always self-sufficient.'

Even so, there are things Janet's partner cannot provide. 'He is less of an intellectual. He can't give me what I used to get on that score. And I am much more educated. But he is an original, and what he says about anything that he reads is instinctive rather than a learned, educated response. Just different, not lesser. Seeing that makes me more tolerant to my ex-husband, more understanding. I see they offer different things. In fact, sometimes, sadly, I am aware that I make more allowances, more effort in this second relationship than I did first time. When you marry very young you do expect your partner to be everything to you. Then, second time round, when you've been through more experiences, you have to admit big differences. There's a past which is different, so you can't bring everything to bear on this relationship. You have to accept these whole dimensions that are yours and that are his. You are already developed and separate so you can't expect to mesh entirely in

56

that romantic way you do when you marry somebody at twenty. Second time round you don't go into it in the belief that you are going to share absolutely everything.'

If everybody thought like Janet, there would be far fewer second divorces. As it is, the failure rate suggests that many people do make the same mistakes twice, even when the partners themselves are very different.

ONLY COMMUNICATE

Whoever is chosen, and for whatever unconscious motives, the ostensible reason for choice is likely to be love, closely followed by strong companionship. In a survey of approximately 250 people carried out by the *Daily Mirror* in 1986, 62% ticked 'deeply in love' and 61% ticked 'good friends' as reasons for marrying a second time.

On the other hand, a Canadian survey of 200 women (in the book *Second Wife, Second Best?*) found that only 33% gave love as the main reason for remarrying, the rest ticking a collection of reasons such as liking/caring, security, societal pressures, loneliness.

There's less emphasis on glamour and more on 'curlers' according to Frank Furstenburg and Graham Spanier in a recent book called *Recycling The Family*. Their 1977–1979 long-term study of married, divorced and remarried people in Pennsylvania revealed less concern about appearance, ambition or status in choice of second partner, and more emphasis on shared interests and stability. This, of course, may simply reflect what people in any stable, satisfying relationship might say.

Respondents claimed that they had found someone who really understood them; or that they had found someone with better communication skills, and this had the effect of making them change in themselves; or the divorce had helped them to experiment and grow. Many had attempted to avoid conflict in a first marriage, men in particular, and more were prepared to view conflict as a normal part of marriage the second time. The majority felt that both made decisions in the current marriage, though more wives were of this opinion than husbands. And in common with other surveys, the men claimed they did more housework than their wives said they did.

All this again sounds like people reading the right books or watching the right television programmes so that they come out with the right answers. When marriage is no longer for worse, but only for better, there is a strong vested interest in seeing the good bits and ignoring the rest. Furstenburg and Spanier also choose to see the good side of this: 'When individuals believe that they have changed and are now married to someone quite different from their former spouse, they have a licence to construct a very different set of marital expectations.' And if it is true that if the new, shared belief consists of better communication, greater trust during disagreements, shared decision-making and more equal allocation of chores then there is a good chance of a shared reality coming out of it. But then, why do second marriages fail, not to mention first ones, since the same willing suspension of disbelief (between the couples) applies to them too?

No doubt expectations are too high and disillusionment creeps in. If more wives than husbands believe that decision-making is shared, and more husbands than wives believe that the housework is shared, sooner or later the truth will out, or at least the couple's perception of it. With communication having such high ratings in the successful relationship scale, the disappointment at finding such gaps may be more than the average married human can bear.

Communication is a much greater attraction for remarriage than sex. The *Daily Mirror* survey had about 10% of its remarrieds ticking sexual attraction as a reason for remarrying. Of course they might have been unwilling to disclose the part sexual attraction played, just in case this was interpreted as treating people as sex objects, but the likelihood is that remarrieds, even more than first marrieds, are reasonably experienced sexually and have had opportunity to establish compatibility beforehand, which inevitably takes some of the urgency out of the situation. All the same, sex is highly important at the beginning, maybe more so in a second marriage if it has been a cause of breakdown in the first. People use it to get out of a marriage, even if only as a result of feeling bored and unloved. A poor sex life gives them the excuse to have an affair—for sexual excitement or revenge. And then the sexual desire for the new person becomes the bonding agent.

When sexual fulfilment first got the full treatment from the experts and the publishing industry, anybody and any marriage judged to be experiencing poor quality sex was deemed to be in need of urgent therapeutic care and attention. Inevitably, some never got it or didn't respond well to it, and a lot of marriages went under, though without the pressure they might have trundled along quite happily with modest aspirations and fewer orgasms. An American *Family Circle* survey in 1979 came to the conclusion that 'neither great sex nor any sex at all is crucial for a happy marriage', having commissioned the Family Therapy Institute of the Western Psychiatric Institute to interview 100 couples of assorted ages, from early twenties to over sixty with marriage duration to match.

We may be doing the same disservice to communication, which like sex can be life-enhancing, but also can be conducted at a low-key level without causing any harm. To most people, communication means talking, sharing thoughts, ideas and opinions, and being able to say things without risking ridicule or rejection. It means feeling understood and *allowed*. Naturally it would have special value in second marriages which have followed a first in which these qualities were felt to be missing.

Ability to talk over problems is one yardstick of communication. In a series of articles on marriage research in the *New York Times* in 1985 and 1986, research work from the University of Denver showed that in unhappy couples, husbands seemed oblivious of their wives' hostility during discussions about problems, though it was obvious to observers. Wives, however, were highly conscious of their husbands' hostility even when it wasn't apparent to the observers. This was probably not a measure of male insensitivity, but of male abhorrence of verbal confrontation, particularly with their all-too-confrontation-happy wives. The latter are better barometers of problems in the marriage, said Dr Howard Markman, who carried out the research, a conclusion that comes as no surprise to anyone.

Male methods of displaying unhappiness can be a little on the

subtle side. Sasha Brookes, a British marriage guidance counsellor, comments on a couple she had been counselling where
the wife had expressed her feeling of deprivation because of her
husband's emotional withdrawal: 'I believed that Dave must
have been experiencing something equally painful, but this did
not seem to be acknowledged . . . It seemed that in family
interaction Dave mainly expressed pain indirectly, through
sighs for example, which though they communicated his
oppression did not allow others to respond, because they did
not make explicit what pain he was feeling. He also heaved sighs
at times when it was difficult to take notice of them, because
something else was going on.'

This too has a familiar ring.

Dr John Gottman, head of research at Illinois University,
found that it is mainly wives in happy marriages who are
comfortable with confrontation, because they find it easy to
switch from conflict to conciliation. Husbands, even happy
ones, are less flexible. And even unhappy wives will continue
the confrontation, putting on the emotional pressure while
husbands withdraw more and more.

Happy couples apparently develop a kind of private language, with subtle cues and private words which observers find
difficult to understand. Unhappy couples appear not to have
this gift—observers were as adept at understanding messages
from wives as were their own husbands. Happy couples also
have a high degree of responsiveness in sharing events of the
day. The absence of responsiveness can lead to heightened
tensions according to Dr Gottman.

This kind of research reflects a change in emphasis among
some psychologists from personality and psychological problems to the nature of the relationship itself—a more behaviourist approach. Conventional psychology still homes in on
childhood experiences and the way these affect ability to choose
a suitable partner. Dr Robert Sternberg of Yale University
considers that high divorce rates are due less to unsuitable
choices than to the fact that the reasons that drew a couple
together matter less as time goes on. Hence, passion is important at first, but then subsides while intimacy and commitment
develop more slowly. He points to intimacy as one of the major

ingredients of success: 'Both partners find it increasingly important to understand each other's wants and needs, to be able to listen to and support each other, and to share common values.'

This is a more subtle and mysterious definition of communication. Why are some couples more adept at achieving intimacy than others? Because they had trusting, secure relationships with their parents, comes the unerring cry from conventional therapists, a claim that is equally subtle and mysterious, all things being possible but not necessarily applicable.

For whatever reasons, some people are happier about self-disclosure than others, and this must have an effect on communication. When both partners are low on self-disclosure, then everybody's happy, and only when there is discrepancy is there also dissatisfaction according to research by Dr B. Davidson published in *The Journal of Marriage and the Family*. But high marital adjustment may accompany what Davidson and fellow researchers called 'a distortion of perception of disclosure to eliminate stress', which sounds rather like the shared make-believes of Furstenburg and Spanier's subjects. When the emotional climate is right, issues like unequal self-disclosure can be adapted to fit it.

Is communication a red herring then, and no more essential to successful relationships than 'high quality' sex? Or is it more important to women, the majority of whom seem to find self-disclosure and intimacy easy and unfrightening achievements?

Dr Ted Huston, University of Texas (*New York Times* again) thinks that men feel emotional closeness through doing things like the gardening or going to the cinema with their wives. This does not go down so well with women, who feel that intimacy depends on talking, especially about the relationship itself. Says Huston, 'The men say, I want to do things with her, and all she wants to do is talk.'

Meanwhile, the women say that it wasn't like that before they were married, and Huston agrees: 'Men put on a big show of interest when they are courting, but after the marriage their actual level of interest often doesn't seem as great. The intimacy of courtship is instrumental for the men, and a way to capture the woman's interest. But that sort of intimacy is not natural for many men.'

The feminist response to this is: Typical! Only when they are after something do they lay on the charm and make an effort to appear interested. Once they have made the conquest the ability is no longer 'natural'. An equally critical male might say that women tend to be too dependent, too caught up in personal relationships, and whereas they are sweetly complying when attention is directed towards them, women become over-demanding when other interests prevail.

There is truth in both. Men do seem to find intimacy difficult to sustain, and even boring at times, no doubt to a great extent because they have been brought up to expect other things from life. Women do tend to put emotional relationships before everything else, and put more effort into making them work. Greater equality between the sexes should make for more flexibility and greater understanding, though not necessarily for the generations busily marrying, divorcing and remarrying at the present time. Even so, John Gottman of Illinois suspects that it's not all nurture, and that men are inherently more vulnerable than women to physical stress from emotional confrontations. This could mean that they might protect themselves from intimacy, which might lead to confrontation.

On the other hand, there are men who are not afraid of intimacy or confrontation, and women who are, which could bring us back to how your father or mother was with you when you were a child. But there is also the importance of learned and repeated personal experience. The person who changes mood quickly will feel the change more acutely than someone who changes slowly, and may even feel greater discomfort because of it. Such a person will experience relief through verbal expression and feel that communication is a useful tool for bringing about change. But try telling that to someone who finds communication difficult and whose natural reaction is extreme discomfort on encountering that verbal expression.

Marital experts generally do not see the contradictions in advocating high communication on the one hand, and cultivating tolerance on the other. We still get the old-fashioned stuff about trying to understand the other party and not making too many demands. Advice columns issue such directives as—don't overreact to your spouse's bad moods . . . rate issues on a scale of 1 to 10 and forgive and forget if the issue falls low . . . don't discuss heated issues before dinner when blood sugar is low . . . try to change the subject . . . live and let live . . .

None of these eminently sensible suggestions would go down at all well as offerings on the altar of the communications god. Indeed, those who find use for them might be forgiven for thinking that they had poor, stilted relationships, according to current standards. Where is the freedom and spontaneity?

Advice columns are mainly addressed to women, who have a high regard for communication. In a sense, the advice is telling them to communicate less in the cause of a better relationship. This happens clearly with some of the techniques used for assertiveness training. People are taught how to make a point without creating a confrontation or encouraging conflict. While the ultimate aim is better communication, it is in effect asking people to expect a little less from others while making more room to accommodate both points of view. Unfortunately, it is women who are most likely to be reading the advice columns in magazines, and it is mainly women who are attracted to assertiveness training courses. Men remain on the outside, neither learning how to communicate more, nor how to communicate better—which may be two very different things.

Social psychologist Michael Argyle has a list of mundane 'rules' that he says people apply to marriage. The top ten are: showing emotional support, sharing news of success, being faithful, creating a harmonious home atmosphere, respecting privacy, keeping confidences, engaging in sex with partner, giving birthday cards and presents, standing up for partner in his or her absence, addressing partner by first name. These rules were based on a consensus of opinion from nearly 1,000 people in four different cultures, but not on gender difference.

While Argyle is for communication, he is definitely against letting it all hang out, doing our own thing, and all those strictures against inhibition that we learned in the permissive Sixties. Being considerate and civilised, and perhaps a little cautious in our communication, makes for greater satisfaction and may even protect any shared delusion of equality and harmony.

Good communication, like good sex, is so easy when it's there, so difficult to attain when it isn't. Sex therapists suggest go-slow techniques, restrictions on touching, etc., to recreate an atmosphere of security, sensitivity and goodwill. A similarly gentle retreat might be more useful for improving communication than increased effort at confrontation or confession, which is the popular mode among many couples, and with many marriage guidance counsellors.

A communication go-slow would include the notion that communication is often an illusion, a kind of wish-fulfilment; that it can operate at times, but lie dormant at others; that self-honesty and self-awareness are more important; that expectation and demand have to be readjusted; and that a personal change of outlook will do more for a relationship than sharing all the anguishes.

In the end, communication is dependent on goodwill, from which all else flows. A second marriage may feel quite different from a first because one has goodwill, and the other lost it. With goodwill goes the kind of tolerance that turns a blind eye, that compensates with a bit of self-deception, and then seals with the honorary title 'communication'. Only when the goodwill breaks down does a second marriage begin to resemble one that has broken down before.

Chapter 4
MEET THE STEPFAMILY

Remarriage is the result of a choice made by adults. Stepfamilies are what they and their children find themselves part of. The conflict of interests is almost always unavoidable. Couples pick each other; children and stepparents normally do not. Whichever way one looks at it, the children come off worst, and knowing this puts their elders in a difficult position. On the one hand, remarrying adults will have a strong emotional investment in their own relationship; on the other, they will have an equally strong emotional investment in being good parents and stepparents. The problem is how to find and keep a reasonable balance between the two.

Of course happy stepfamilies exist, but they will have had to get through even more obstacles than first-time-married families. There are many subtle contradictions and complexities to negotiate and stages of development to work through either consciously or at a more instinctive level.

The stepfamily is an odd animal. It can include children from both previous marriages or from one. Any of the children may live permanently under one roof, or part-time under another. There may be children of the new union. And an ex-partner might remarry and produce further half-sisters and brothers. No wonder researchers today tend to talk of 'reconstituted' or 'blended' families—words unfortunately reminiscent of artificial foods but somewhat appropriate nevertheless.

One problem for the stepfamily is that as an institution it has no clear identity of its own, and tries instead to emulate non-step families. In a widely-quoted paper, 'Remarriage as an Incomplete Institution', sociologist Andrew Cherlin discusses the absence of adequate guidelines to deal with the complex new family structures. Some of the 'non-institutionalised' problems he refers to are: competing interests of parents, how children should address stepparent or other members of his or her family, incest among members of the stepfamily, lack of guidelines on how to behave with ex-partner.

Rather than face this daunting set of shortcomings, couples tend to make remarriages look as much like first marriages as possible. Muriel and Robin Blandford of the Stepfamily Association find that families will go to endless trouble to disguise their identity. 'They will move house, change the children's names, do anything to appear the normal, original nuclear family,' says Muriel. 'Any stepfamily is formed through some kind of loss somewhere along the line, and there is also this wanting to cover the sense of injury, to cover up the damage.'

Various researches into stepfamilies show that integration is better if the previous spouse has died rather than divorced. It is also better when the remarried couple have a child of their own. Fathers without custody of their own children do not relate to stepchildren as well as bachelors. Stepmothers relate best to young children. Stepmother/stepdaughter relations are the most problematic.

Perhaps the most important finding is that children of divorce function best if they are able to maintain satisfactory contact with both parents and with their original family network. For many people, it is here, more than anywhere else, that the conflict between being adult-centred and child-centred is most difficult to resolve. Establishing a new relationship is not helped when an ex-partner and ex-parents-in-law have to be taken into account for the sake of the children.

The findings above are part of a summary of work on stepfamilies included in a book called *The Family Life Cycle*. Editors Monica McGoldrick and Elizabeth Carter see stepfamilies as having to work through a developmental process where the rules and boundaries are unclear. This is true not only for the adults in their role as stepparent or custodial parent, but also in the way they conduct their relationship with each other.

THE SEVEN STAGES

There has been an attempt to specify the developmental process. Gestalt therapist Patricia Papernow describes seven stages

66

of development, in a paper called *The Stepfamily Cycle*: 1 Fantasy, 2 Assimilation, 3 Awareness, 4 Mobilization, 5 Action, 6 Contact and 7 Resolution.

The first stage, Fantasy, is fairly easy to pinpoint. It is the stage of the romantic rescue, when a prospective stepparent has high hopes of an instant cure for the family's past unhappinesses. Then comes the rude awakening, stage 2, Assimilation. Writing of this, Papernow says: 'The stepparent's feelings of jealousy, resentment and rejection, and the biological parent's feelings of grief, guilt and fear of another loss (of the new partner) are nobody's favourite and are more easily denied than acknowledged.'

This gives way to the Awareness stage, when the couple begin to understand what has been happening, though the subject of the children might still be too raw for discussion between them.

Often, says Papernow, a real shift to stage 4, Mobilization, takes place when there is an 'infusion of support from someone or something outside the couple relationship', meaning another stepparent who has been through it, or a book which clarifies stepfamily struggles, or a knowledgeable therapist. This stage triggers a genuine restructuring of the family. It may mean the stepparent insisting on greater detachment from a demanding ex-spouse, new rules about preserving privacy as a couple, some changes in family routine and discipline.

If it sounds like fireworks, it is: 'In many families, this ushers in a period of conflict and chaos as highly charged differences become aired for the first time.' The unlucky stepparent seems to have to do most of the initiating work, since she or he has most to gain, while the biological parent suffers from conflicting loyalties.

Stage 5, Action, implies articulating personal needs and finding workable solutions to issues like discipline or who goes where at Christmas. The biological parent may take a back seat, while stepparent and stepchild come to grips with each other, possibly even behaving as allies at times against the biological parent.

Finally, there are the Contact and Resolution stages, with increasing intimacy and trust between the various members of what must surely be a battle-scarred family. Papernow gives a subtitle to the Contact stage: 'Now that we're alone together, who are you anyway?' Everybody is talking and listening, and the shouting is presumably over. A family can now accept a stepmother as someone who can contribute something special in her own right, such as helping with choosing clothes or introducing the children to music. A stepfather can be someone who is especially good at sport or maths, or is particularly patient and calm when there are rows. She or he becomes an 'intimate outsider', someone to confide in, someone to act as a genuine mediator with a biological parent.

All this takes time. Some researchers say it takes about two years for the problem of discipline to resolve itself and for stepfathers to become equal with their wives in their management of stepchildren. Others say that the first three to four years are the make or break ones, and though Papernow's stages include some overlapping and slow and fast moves, she considers the families take about four years to get to stage 5, Action, after which development is faster and more positive.

It does sound rather like slow and painful work, and yet in many areas of life we are readily prepared to forgo immediate pleasure for the sake of some distant goal. We may study for years, undertake work involving long and arduous hours, take up gruelling training or endure hardship in order to pass exams, gain promotion, produce works of art, break records, explore hidden terrains. In one most important area of our lives, human relationships, we expect and hope for instant satisfaction. But it is a sad irony that stepparents, who in some cases may not have tried hard enough to make a go of a first marriage, have to work doubly hard in a second.

Therapists base their findings on people who seek help, rather than those who feel they are managing well on their own, and undoubtedly many stepfamilies negotiate their stages of development with comparatively little strain. Elsa Ferri, of the National Children's Bureau, found that two-thirds of teenagers living with stepparents thought they had a good relationship with them, taking her sample of about 600 from the long-term study of all children born in Britain in one week in March, 1958. An overview of American research by Jo Pink and Karen Smith

Wampler revealed a mixed bag of reports, with some step-families functioning as well as first-married families.

COURTING-COUPLES

When two adults focus their attention on each other, what they want most of all is to be alone together. When one or both have children, this may not be very easy. We no longer live in an age in which there is disapproval of pre-marital sex, but we do have anxieties about how much adult sexuality our children should be exposed to, and we have a desire to protect ourselves against those anxieties.

Of course, children need a certain amount of protection too, but motives can easily get muddled so that there is not so much protection going on as deception and delusion. On the one hand, there is the need to keep the adult relationship private, which is perfectly reasonable for a couple going through a period of discovery: on the other, there is the difficulty of keeping it private but not secret. At what stage is it appropriate to tell children? The time may easily be too soon, so that they begin making predictions about their future when in fact the relationship never actually comes to anything. Often it is too late, and children are given little preparation for a wedding in a few weeks time or a new 'uncle' who is going to live with mum, either way an arrangement that will have a profound effect on their lives.

It is possible to be relaxed and open, simply by introducing a new partner as a friend, when he or she is still just that, and by making it easy for children to ask questions and answering them in a straightforward fashion as the relationship does, or does not, develop. But this seems exceedingly difficult to do.

It is at this point that one has to ask: who are we really protecting? Is it our children—or ourselves, from embarrassment, from facing awkward facts, from our own doubts, from our children's criticisms? The irony is that this self-protection creates an atmosphere where no questions can be asked and children are left in a kind of limbo, having to resort to guess-work among themselves. The absence of questions may lead adults to believe that children are blissfully ignorant or totally accepting, but we have only to project ourselves into the situation to appreciate the curiosity, insecurity and excitement engendered by sheer lack of information.

Bob, the architect, who sort of slid into his first marriage, slid out of it by going to live with Sylvia without saying much to his children, then aged seven and nine. 'I was often away for weeks at a time anyway, so I said I had this room in a flat, and as far as they were concerned it was a separate room. The kids came over for tea a few months later, and I showed them the flat and introduced them to Sylvia. And my daughter said, "You don't sleep in this little room, you sleep in the big bed with Sylvia." They seemed to accept it immediately.' Well, they probably had a good idea already.

Parents are often surprised when they learn how perceptive children can be about a new partner. Chrissie, whose husband had left her so abruptly after a seemingly idyllic marriage, had introduced several boyfriends to her children. 'I could see they were relieved when I brought Mark home. They said he was nice and sensible, and it is true, he is loving and patient with them. I hadn't really thought about it before, but I suppose they saw every boyfriend as a potential partner, and the last one had been such a boy, whereas this one had children of his own.'

Sometimes, the encounter one dreads turns out to be a lot easier than expected. Janet, who left her husband and his comfortable life abroad, recalls how her children came across Sam, the man she now lives with.

'I kept him very much away from the children at first, because I wanted this relationship to be something special for me. So he never stayed over and barely came in to pick me up. Then one night we went to a party and we got massively drunk and just fell into bed, and I hadn't bothered to lock the door. And in the morning I came to and said, Oh the kids, and then the door opened and this little face put its head round the door. Sam was so alarmed, he thought it was going to traumatise them for life to find a man in the bed, instead of which these big brown eyes confronted him with interest . . . I mean the excitement of finding a person, and a man to boot, in the house. Sam pulled the sheet up over his face, but my daughter said, hallo, who are you? She was four.'

An older child would have been more discreet, more circumspect, listening from his or her bedroom till the man could be heard quietly closing the front door as he left the house. Questions would not have been expressed in words, only in thoughts, with no help made available.

The double protection of our children and ourselves blocks our ability to think clearly and take sensible action. It also diminishes our children. If we demand too little of their understanding and compassion it is no wonder that they appear to us ungrateful and self-centred as they grow older.

Adolescents, for instance, have a reputation for disliking any display of sexual affection in an older generation, possibly seeing it as ridiculous, embarrassing or encroaching on their own territory. In western society we have become so conditioned to the 'sensitivity' of teenagers that we have learned to be deferential to them and unassertive about our own needs. There are times—and this is one of them—for a different approach. It would not hurt for them to be told sympathetically but firmly that sex was invented long before they were and should be available to all. They need to understand the importance of this new relationship, not only because it might offer them advantages (this only reinforces the selfish view) but because it brings happiness to their parent.

THE ROMANTIC RESCUE

Once the news of a new relationship is made public, a couple with children are likely to acquire youthful chaperones. Adolescents may want to keep out of the way, but younger children create babysitting problems. They have to be entertained, taken on outings, given treats. When a remarriage is in the making, the children have to be courted too.

There can be a certain novelty in this, and of course a challenge. A couple in love and full of optimism wish to please one another. They are prepared to love their partner's children and are often determined to do so, mistakenly thinking that if the will is there everything good must surely follow. Now is the time when Papernow's Fantasy stage manifests itself. The new partner might have a vision of a romantic rescue—a woman taking over motherless children, a man becoming the provider for a fatherless family.

This is another part of the delusion. A stepparent cannot replace a natural parent, regardless of whether that person is alive or dead, is seen as villain or inadequate. Love does not automatically follow an offer of optimistic goodwill, though continued offers of goodwill are necessary, no matter what the rebuffs. The romantic rescue is inappropriate for children mourning a loss and can lead to what may feel to them like a take-over.

After the death of a parent, there is no guarantee that a young child will welcome a new partner for the surviving parent, though teenagers and older children might well feel a sense of relief. A young child may not be able to encompass what seems like a deep disloyalty and could feel anger towards anyone who might appear to want to erase the memory of the dead parent.

The newcomer to the family may be accepted at one level, but looks can be deceptive. A hitherto one-parent family may have developed into a close-knit group with special loyalties and rules of behaviour. An outsider is an intruder who needs to tread carefully and slowly in order to gain real acceptance. Early confidences from a child might be the real thing, but they might as easily be an attempt to do the right thing and be a compensation for negative feelings. If the adults are fooled—and they often are—it's because they want to be.

Ann Mitchell in her book *Children In The Middle*, found that children were less appreciative of their parents' new partners than the parents themselves had indicated. Some parents did not seem to be aware of their children's antipathy to the new partner. The reasons are fairly obvious. If parents waited for children to choose their partners for them, they would get just one nomination, and we all know who that would be.

The 1975 Children's Act made it possible for joint custody to be offered to stepparents, a move that of course aids the illusion of family unity. It is possible to rewrite family history even more thoroughly by adoption, which may well have a point with very young children, especially if their biological parent is dead. But if the parent is alive, family history may eventually rewrite itself yet again.

Children of remarriage shouldn't be encouraged to hide their identity unless there is a very good reason for doing so. They should be able to acknowledge a stepparent easily. Too often, in social situations they may find people referring to the stepparent as 'your father', as if it would be impolite or tactless to admit to the existence of a stepfather. This makes it difficult for children to carry the knowledge easily.

Lillian Messinger, a remarriage researcher in Toronto, found that children in seventy remarriages who were required to respond to the parent's new mate as though he or she were the 'real' parent, showed guilt, hostility, rebellion or withdrawal. Even children who called the new spouse by his or her first name would still introduce this person to their friends as 'my father' or 'my mother', no doubt to avoid problems and tiresome explanations.

The question of different surnames can cause embarrassment in some families, which is one reason why a stepparent might seek adoption. Schools and other institutions have a way of drawing attention to names that don't seem to fit the conventions, and if they could be more matter-of-fact about them, everyone would feel more comfortable. As it is, stepfamilies have to find the way that feels most easy to them without distorting reality.

'Sociological parenting'—the stepparent taking on the role of parent when he (mostly he) no longer sees his own children or when he knows there will not be any children of his own from the new marriage—is something creative and good in its own right. But it can never break the bond between a child and the biological parent, though other things like neglect, absence or indifference certainly can.

This may be very tough for a man who feels responsible for his stepchildren, and in the main supports them. One of the suggestions put forward by the Law Commission in 1985 in relation to changes in child care law is to have a system whereby the divorced and widowed could appoint stepparents as guardians. This would put the sharing of parental powers and responsibilities on a firmer footing and provide a proper sense of status for the stepparent.

It does not always follow that children will accept someone as

73

a stepparent simply because they have known him or her previously as a friend of the family. Norman and June had known each other several years before they decided to marry, and during that time Norman and his first wife had visited June with the children. Says June, 'The children knew me as an aunty figure, and that was all right. But then Norman moved out and we decided that I should see them. They came to my house and I cooked them some lunch. They were three and seven at the time. They were all right when we picked them up, but on the way back the older one was very sick and it was all going through her mind. We hadn't realised how upset she was. From then on we took them out once or twice a month and we had no problems at all. They just accepted me. It didn't seem to occur to them to do anything else.'

At the same time, June admits that visits now are stressful. The younger child wets the bed. The older one cries sometimes before a visit, sometimes after. There are problems over discipline. It was easier to play down the problems in those early days, when there were so many issues, pleasant and unpleasant, fighting for attention. It is always easier to take quiescent children at face value if they offer the opportunity, and to ignore the negative signals.

Janet coped with this dilemma by employing what could be called a sensitive optimism. 'I think I was a controlling influence by thinking positively . . . but of course you've still got to give space for the other voice to come through. I wouldn't have wanted to create an atmosphere where the children couldn't say anything critical.'

There's a fine line between creating an atmosphere of censorship and pushing optimism, and it comes from acknowledging the doubts mentally if not verbally, so there is room for others involved to voice their opinions too.

THE AWFUL WEEKENDS

Over 5% of all children under sixteen in Britain live with a stepparent. For many it means taking on two sets of families: the one they live with most of the time, which is more likely to include their mother, and the one they might visit at weekends or for holidays, which may come complete with another step-parent and even stepsiblings.

Most children want to see their absent parent and often enjoy having stepbrothers and sisters. But the word that can come up after a visit is 'phew', a letting off of steam caused by the strain of attempting to behave impeccably and not always succeeding. This in itself is not so terrible. We all have to make an effort at being on our best behaviour at times. The reaction even indicates a degree of humour and a trust in the tolerance of the family of main residence that they will not take advantage of the admission. You can't say 'phew' to a parent who is only too ready to pounce at the merest hint of criticism against the ex-spouse. But it is a pity that the non-custodial parent and new partner, together with the children, can have such awful weekends.

If they are really awful, there may be tears and vomiting to express feelings too strong to be satisfied by 'phew'. And then of course, the custodial parent can start on the heavy stuff, perhaps by denying access, which could lead to a court order if the other home seems that unsuitable.

Such a move might be justified, but there is a good chance that the children are telling tales to make trouble—anything to drive a wedge between the new couple and so get mother or father back for themselves. If this sounds foolishly self-destructive, it is as well to remember that catty stories about the other half of the family are often what adults want to hear.

The awful weekends occur because nobody is sure they really want them, though, equally, no one knows what to put in their place. Children of course simply want their parents to be reunited and, especially in adolescence, resent being told what to do and where to spend their time. Non-custodial parents feel they ought to see their children but sometimes don't want to see them and then feel guilty and insist on doing so to make up for the feeling.

Children in any kind of family are not too keen on visits to relatives, no matter how much loved, unless there are interesting things to do or interesting people to see, and not every non-custodial parent can lay on a sandpit or children of a similar age group or even a video. (The latter would surely provoke

75

criticism back home—'all they do when they go there is watch television'.)

It is the anxiety built into the situation that makes for the difficulties. The adults are watchful in case the wrong stories get back, and even good weekends, really happy times with lots of fun and distractions, could make a child feel guilty because of betrayed loyalties.

The underlying problem is jealousy and rivalry between the adults. Too often, the custodial parent does not want a child to get on too well in the other home. And in the other home, the stepparent overdoes the welcome and at the same time watches for signs of unsatisfactory behaviour in the children which could be construed as bad parenting.

The sense of rivalry leads to stepmothers buying clothes and providing treats to win affection, mothers resenting the intrusion and fearing they cannot compete, and both rationalising their actions in order to disguise their naked and uncomfortable competitiveness.

And what of the children in all this? They may enjoy the outings and the extra pocket money and the good times, but the last thing they really want to do is to feel compelled to make choices to appease the needs of the adults in charge of them. Despite the stresses of a broken home, children can be very generous. They can show that it's possible to avoid torn loyalties. Ann Mitchell reports on several young people who had good relations with new partners of their non-custodial parents.

One girl said of her stepmother, 'I used to think she was taking my Dad away. Now we get on great. I turn to her with all my problems. She wanted me to call her Mum, but I didn't want that.' Ann Mitchell found that new partners of non-custodial parents were rarely looked upon as stepparents. More often they were considered a friend of the parent, even when the couple were married. The attitude is shown clearly in this comment from a ten-year-old boy quoted in *Ms* magazine: 'My stepmother, I think of her as a friend. I can tell her certain things that I can tell my friends but . . . I would never consider her as my mother. You know, I don't think anybody could take the place of my mother even if my mother died.'

This attitude seems an obvious solution for children, and

works best when the adults involved can genuinely feel that there is some advantage in having two sets of parents, where friendship as well as love is offered. Too often, both parents and stepparents feel and reveal that they are giving second-best, are trying to make amends or even trying to go one better. The other family is the enemy, an unfortunate mistake from the past that would be forgotten were it not for the presence of the children.

DEGREES OF CONTACT

Some newly-established couples do everything to discourage a high degree of contact with the non-custodial parent. 'It only upsets the child,' they say by way of rationalisation, though lack of display of upset is no guarantee of its absence. On the whole, evidence from research suggests that a high degree of contact with the biological father is good for everyone, especially, oddly enough, for the relationship between adolescents and their stepfathers. 'High' means more than once a week; 'medium' is twice a month; 'low' is less than once a month.

'High' is more likely to mean that parents have joint custody, an arrangement that is slowly growing in popularity. Unlike American joint custody arrangements, where children might remain in the matrimonial home and parents alternate living with them, or a child might live for half a year with one parent and then move for the other half to live with the other parent, in Britain joint custody usually means that a child lives mainly with one parent (usually mother), but access to the other parent is regular and of some duration, perhaps every weekend and holidays, perhaps some days in the week too. Joint custodial parents often arrange that they live near enough to each other for this kind of arrangement to work conveniently.

Fathers with joint custody tend to provide fewer outings and treats, and create a real home for their children. They are more concerned about control and discipline and about the emotional development of their children.

Ian, the teacher, who has joint custody and finds himself increasingly in charge of his children, is a case in point. 'I would certainly not expect my ex-wife's partner to be in charge of their moral welfare. They are with me often enough to accept my standards and values. Their mother would always discuss school progress or any decisions about their behaviour with me, even though we don't always see eye to eye.'

Alternating between two homes tends to be regarded with suspicion, sometimes to the point of absurdity. A legal report in the *Guardian* explained one situation as follows:

'An arrangement under which a child of nearly nine had no single settled home, but lived alternate weeks with each of her divorced parents, was *prima facie* wrong, and the fact that the arrangement had subsisted for five years with no apparent detriment to the child did not justify its continuance . . . The Court of Appeal granted care and control to the mother and ordered that the father should have reasonable access.'

Care and control still allows the father custody, which means that he can decide on issues such as schooling.

This may have been more satisfactory from the mother's point of view since it was she who sought the change, but does not necessarily mean that the child benefitted. Perhaps nobody asked the child. It is quite likely that he or she might enjoy a whole week in one home, and then the same in another if both homes are welcoming and provide acceptable accommodation, and if parents cooperate in understanding his or her need. Odd weekends may be considerably less satisfactory.

Martin Richards of the University of Cambridge Child Care and Development Group counters any suggestion that high contact or alternating living arrangements cause confusion in children. 'Children are adaptable. They have the ability to perceive and cope with different household patterns. The Courts see a child as having one home, and to me that is fundamentally wrong. They say that most kids live in one home with two parents, but that's not the comparison to make. With divorce, you're living in one home with one parent and seeing the other parent only occasionally. Is it better to have that than children living in two homes?'

All the care and concern about the children may be less to the point than another factor, which is to do with the adults. As Martin Richards says, 'Continued contact with the second parent is likely to stir up hostility because it violates the widespread belief that a clean break at divorce is the only way for adults to manage their feelings.' It's a question of the interests of the adults and the children being at odds again: adults may want to minimise contact in order to minimise their anger; children want to remain in contact with the people they love.

If there is any doubt that children can put one and one together, even when divorced, then take note of these comments which emerged from a discussion with a group of fifteen-year-olds in a comprehensive school:

'My mother can be angry about my father, and then I feel I should be too. Sometimes I feel more sympathetic to one, sometimes to the other.'

'Often it's the dad who's banished. My father comes to see us occasionally, and we want to see him. But I know my mother doesn't really want us to see him.'

'I feel guilty because I don't answer my father's letters—it would be disloyal to my mum. I wish he'd go away and forget us, it would be less trouble. But I also admit that it upsets me if he doesn't write. I don't really know what I want of him.'

Confusion may be greater when there is banishment than when contact is acknowledged and accepted. Children can take parental conflict in their stride when they know they have a licence to make contact regularly and consistently. Those in families where access is difficult are known to be less well adjusted than those with easy contact. Those who have no contact at all are considered to be poorly adjusted in their general behaviour.

Not every family would benefit from joint custody or regular access—a parent with severe behaviour problems might justify brief and well-supervised visits at most—but the case for high contact is strong, and ultimately makes for better relationships all round.

QUESTIONS OF DISCIPLINE

There is no area more fraught for stepparenting than discipline. On the one hand, a stepmother will try to please, on the other she may find herself defending standards she feels strongly about, knowing that doing so may jeopardise her longed-for family unity. A stepfather might perhaps make respect a higher priority than wanting to please his stepchildren, and thus risk alienating them.

Chrissie has experienced the dilemma of wanting to please and wanting to establish certain standards of behaviour with her stepchildren. 'I am quite strict with my children in some ways. They know where the limits are. Mark's children have been much more spoiled. I've said to Mark, I want to treat them the same way as I treat mine because that's only fair. But on the other hand I can't help being critical about not eating food with fingers and not saying thank you when you've given them a present. That sort of thing. It's silly, I know. You start off by making a joke of it, but then it builds up until you have an almighty row. I have such a chip on my shoulder about this, in case they think I'm an old bag.'

Guilt does not enhance the process, but then neither does angry justification, which is the way some stepmothers tackle the problem. This is where blaming the biological mother comes in. It is easier than blaming the children themselves and provides an outlet for otherwise suppressed rivalry and jealousy. Talking to stepmothers, one might easily get the impression that biological mothers are sluts, disorganised, unable or unwilling to control their children, unnecessarily extravagant and entirely impractical. These defects, of course, will have driven their husbands into the arms of someone less sluttish and disorganised, someone who, now, not only has to try to make amends, but has to help pay out maintenance money to this unworthy spendthrift.

There may be some truth in such ideas. A failing marriage can cause depression in one or both partners. Separation may increase the depression, especially in a woman on her own having to cope with small children. She may be demoralised, which makes her disorganised, or unaccustomed to dealing with the children on her own. She may have been the more reasonable of the two parents, compensating for a stressed husband who let out his tension by over-disciplining. She may be unaccustomed to handling money. It may also be that as parents they had different standards, or thresholds of tolerance, regarding cleanliness and order, which is one reason why the marriage broke up.

Children staying in a stepparent's house on a regular but fairly infrequent basis have to learn the new rules of the household, which can feel like a betrayal towards the parent they normally live with. They may perceive that here is a danger area, with scope for rebellion and confrontation, or make it a testing ground to find out how acceptable they are to their parent and new partner.

There is no doubt that feelings run high. The issues may seem trivial—wiping feet on the mat before entering the house, washing hands before meals, tidiness, swearing, watching television, eating habits, saying thank you, being careful with pocket money, changing underwear—but they can cause an enormous amount of dissent, not to mention conflict, if a stepmother has her own children living with her, and they accept stricter standards. This is where the wicked stepmother myth really comes into its own, and being fantasy, the unfairness gets distorted. Cinderella received harsher treatment than her stepsisters, though she, of course, was blameless. In real life, children, like adults, rarely are quite so perfect.

The reason for all the rule-making is that it establishes boundaries and makes for identification. Rule-making helps to create a feeling of unity and being in control. It defines what is acceptable and what is not within a group, and then calls everything inside the magic circle O K and everything outside it taboo. In this case, it is an attempt to make the stepfamily 'normal', meaning the way it would be if it weren't a stepfamily. We do need rules for stepfamilies, if only because two different households will have different ideas of what is allowable or tolerable, but we may be using the wrong ones.

Discipline and the making of new rules occur in stages 4 and 5, Mobilization and Action, according to the Papernow theory. Papernow herself suggests that a way to cope is to avoid a right and wrong approach. 'The differences between two families (should) be described without connotations . . . "In this family it's O K to swear, but only three hours of television per day. In your Mom's house you can't swear and you can watch as much television as you like." . . .' Some families may have no relaxation of rules, i.e., no swearing, no television, but presumably one can be inventive over this. The aim is to establish a set of expectations that are considered acceptable by the household, but at the same time to acknowledge that they are arbitrary. Most of us acquire our domestic habits from our own biological families, but sometimes adopt alternatives as a kind of rebellion or to define our own autonomy.

David Mills, a psychotherapist writing on stepfamily development, suggests that stepparents should engage in a trial period in which they do not make direct requests themselves but make it clear that they are speaking for the biological parent when requesting certain behaviour. This means prefacing remarks with, 'Your parent said you should . . .' and even . . . 'Would you ask your children to . . .' when adults and children are present, which also means that parent and stepparent will have got their act together behind the scenes. Mills reports that some couples object to the idea on the basis that it appears to make a split in the family, but that after trying it for a week, they experience great relief. 'Now, however, conflicts which were previously expressed between stepparent and child begin to break out between parent and stepparent.' On the whole, that should be easier to deal with.

Mills also makes a suggestion which contradicts most people's idea of what is fair. He points out that most of us have different rules for children of different ages or special needs, so why not different rules for children of different households?

This is an exceedingly tough proposition to put into action. How do you let the stepchildren drink, smoke, swear, when yours are not allowed these luxuries? How can one child be absolved from washing hands before meals when others at the same table are given to understand that it is compulsory? Taking into account different ages and needs, and the way these are explained to children, it is just about possible to explain why special allowances are made, though it would take a saint to do so without being patronising and possibly insulting to the biological parent. Nevertheless, the idea is a useful one. It implicitly assumes that the stepfamily is something wider and more variable than the conventional nuclear family.

The restricted norms can be disregarded, and new ones developed.

A great deal of pain, confusion and rivalry could be avoided if all the adults got together to work out the rules. This could still mean different standards and ideals, but it could also mean a greater amount of respect for each household. As it is, children learn too much about differences and intolerances between adults—which is rather worse than omitting to wash hands before meals, or swearing.

Chapter 5
PARENTAL PRESSURES

Biological parents as well as stepparents are touched by many conflicting interests in remarriage. Almost always, they are aiming to be fair and loving and decent with the children in their charge, but many things can get in the way of these ideals.

The wicked stepmother of fairytale fame may be the subject of partial misrepresentation. Two of the most notorious, those inherited by Snow White and Cinderella, appear to be victims of insecurity, the one over-bothered about ageing, the other concerned to marry off her two ugly, charmless daughters. This does not condone their jealousy or their callousness towards the motherless children in their charge, but it does raise interesting questions about their relationships with their husbands, the biological fathers of the maligned children. They are conspicuously absent from the domestic scene, as are so many fathers in real life. Well-meaning fathers who find a new mother for their children are perhaps tempted to feel that they have done their bit and can wash their hands of the details.

Cruel stepfathers occur in fact perhaps more than they occur in fiction. Recent findings about sexual abuse and violence towards children suggest that there is a particular danger with some stepfathers, who are often young, unemployed and feel little responsibility towards the children of the women they are living with. Fortunately, the majority of stepfathers are caring and responsible, but it is still mothers and stepmothers who feel the strain of 'reconstituted' families.

In remarriage, the majority of children stay with their mothers—only 10–15% of fathers have sole custody. But fathers remarry, and their wives often also feel the responsibility, even if they act as stepmothers only one weekend in two or for a holiday period. Women take the burden on themselves

84

and everyone else is relieved about it. Here is someone who recognises the problems, will easily accept the guilt and therefore is easily blamed. Fathers and stepfathers tend to stay out of the firing line, pleading innocence and ignorance.

Though children feature so strongly in remarriages, the present trends are towards an increase in childlessness if women continue to postpone having children. One might see a typical situation in which a couple live together or marry and postpone having a family, then they divorce, and by the time the woman remarries she may feel too old to have children or may have difficulty in conceiving. Again, because of age and financial factors, only a small minority of remarried couples have three sets of children, i.e. from both previous marriages and from the new marriage.

MOTHER FIGURES

Inevitably, mothers have the most difficult time in most remarriages. They can experience torn loyalties and fear of losing the second partner, as noted in Papernow's Assimilation stage in the previous chapter. There is an added guilt in that they know that they are choosing a new partner primarily for themselves. The statutory selfless standard required of motherhood is being eroded.

Margie, who met and married Graham very soon after her first husband moved out, has three of her four children living with them. The children were aged five, twelve and thirteen when the couple married six years ago, and Maria, the twelve-year-old, hated the idea of Graham as a stepfather. Says Margie, 'She idolised her dad. I was torn between understanding her feelings about her father and not understanding her feelings towards Graham. But I never felt it would come between us. Although blood is thicker than water, and obviously they're my children and I've got to protect them, basically Graham comes first because, well, my kids are gong off one day, so if I put all my love and affection into them, it leaves little for my husband.'

The slight muddle in the last sentence reveals some of the conflict. It sounds more respectable to put the onus on the fact that the children will leave, even when you have acknowledged the strength of your own needs.

Being at the centre of family life, mothers tend to want to integrate. When they are stepmothers, they may feel the urge to make an extended happy family with their new partners' children, even if they only turn up for the odd weekend. Graham's children were seven and eight when his first marriage ended, and Margie wanted to welcome them and encouraged her own children to do so. 'It would have been lovely because they all fitted in age, but my kids have run out of energy and they don't bother any more. It's a shame. But they were more of a threat to us than my own children, though we never see them. There 's still tension with them even now, six years later.'

Chrissie, having found that her children, then seven and nine, took to her second husband very quickly, sees a cemented relationship now. 'I've tried very hard not to let any idea of his being their father creep in, but because he is dependable and solid and he does so much for them like taking them shopping and picking them up from parties, I wonder . . .'

Chrissie's husband has two children of similar age who live very nearby with their mother, and they visit regularly. 'All of the children get on amazingly well, but I am not half so tolerant to Mark's children as he is to mine, and my youngest can be unspeakably revolting at times. They have been brought up in a very different way. Mine have been smothered with love and kisses, Mark's are not so outgoing. They don't want to be too friendly with me because they might feel it is detracting from the love they give their mother. But it is hurtful and I do resent it sometimes when they don't show me affection after I've offered it to them.'

The problem of giving love which is not welcomed is clearly a part of Papernow's Fantasy stage described in the previous chapter. In some circumstances, trying to give love might be a form of compensation for guilt at having entered the step-children's lives uninvited.

Chrissie's ex-husband has remarried and is now living in England again. 'My children love seeing their father but they don't like their stepmother. They are very loyal to him though, and they say don't be horrid when I make a sarcastic dig about either of them. I've said I'm sorry. I've had to explain about making a slip and having prejudices. I have to admit I don't want my children to love their stepmother more than me. The children go there every other weekend. She is very rich and so they go skiing with them, things like that.'

So subtle rivalries evolve. Could this stepmother win Chrissie's children's affections with her special treats? Relations between mother and stepmother are often strained because of financial arrangements. If stepmothers feel as if they are unwilling contributors to mothers with feckless spending habits, then mothers feel they can't compete in spending power with self-sufficient money-earning stepmothers who could seduce the children and steal their love with gifts and treats, as Chrissie has revealed above.

Stepmothers in this situation might see things quite differently. Sylvia, married to the architect Bob, not only regards herself as someone more liberated and worldly than Bob's first wife, she also wants to emphasise this with the children, and uses her spending power and sense of sophistication to do so, restrained only by a sense of propriety.

'I find it very sad for the kids, because they get a very narrow upbringing there. When they come to us, they like our style. I want to show them the world. I like taking them to Disneyworld and skiing. I suppose I do and I don't want to turn them against their mother. I don't want them to become like her but I know that it's unhealthy to do anything to turn them against the sort of life she's bringing them up to lead. They don't get exposure to classical music because she doesn't like it. I don't say anything about that but I do talk to them about the history of music and why it's important. Their mother is very greedy as far as money goes, and I think the way she sees it is that the kids will do quite well out of me, so though she might feel I spoil them or I'm showing off, she also quite welcomes it.'

Then there's a question of taste . . . 'I don't like the way she dresses them. The boy's OK because he wears jeans. The girl, well it's less of a problem than it's going to be. Their mother doesn't dress them with any flair, so I buy her the odd thing that's fashionable and these are style-conscious kids, so by the time the girl is a teenager there will be more of a problem.'

The competitiveness and anger are very near the surface here. At the same time, people try to give what they can, and in this case Sylvia is giving her wealth and experience. They would be more acceptable gifts if she stopped trying to compete. The only easy way to offer something different is to judge it simply as different, with no strings.

Sandra, who was so hurt when Steven wavered between her and his ex-wife, still feels certain insecurities with her stepsons, though she and Steven have been married for ten years. 'Dougie was only five when Steven finally left. The boys came to us every other weekend. I know that a week after Steven left, his wife had this person move in, and they eventually married, but you do dread them blaming you for splitting up their parents. I've talked more openly about it with Dougie than with the older one because he wanted to. The boys have said things to me that make me feel that their mother is not hostile to me any more, but I also know that she doesn't acknowledge that I have a relationshp with them. But I know, certainly with Dougie, who's seventeen now, that we are important to each other. But he did forget my birthday, and it's silly but I have been very hurt about it when he's forgotten in the past. I've told them both. It would have helped if their mother had reminded them. There's no language for being a stepparent, no "happy birthday, stepmother" cards . . .'

There is a new type of second family emerging which is quite unlike the situations described above. When a woman lives with a new partner rather than marying him, she may not wish to create a new family, or may respect her partner's wish to remain fairly detached. As in Harriet's case, she may own her home, be the major wage-earner, and see her relationshp with a man as something that is solely for herself, while her son belongs to another part of her life.

'Tim, the man I live with, is very good with my son, not trying to be a father, nor an uncle. It would be a terrible mistake to take the place of a perfectly good father, which my ex-husband is. Our son was totally innocent in all this, so why should he suffer? All he wants is for his mummy and daddy to live together in peace and harmony, and just because we've made a mess of it doesn't mean that he shouldn't be our son. He is not my property. He loves us both very much and we have joint custody. My ex-husband bought a house just round the corner, which was one of the things we decided to do when we separated.'

Janet, who has been living with her present partner for four years, having bought a house with him, thinks that he does not want to take on a fatherly role with her three children, now aged eight, nine and ten. 'Sam has never wanted children of his own. He's more a nice uncle-y figure. My oldest child understands quite consciously that if he is good for me and makes me happy then he's a good person to have around. She takes him very much as "mummy's friend", and that's just fine because I don't want it to interrupt her relationship with her dad. I think that's the most you could ask for really.'

FATHER FIGURES

Over 85% of divorced fathers do not have custody of their children. For many, this is a severe deprivation. They do not see their children as often as they would wish. But research from Furstenburg and Spanier in Pennsylvania showed that 50% of children in disrupted families had not seen their non-custodial parent in five years. Once a week visits were rare; birthdays and holidays were more common. In Britain, some 40% of children have no contact with a parent within two years of the divorce when the parent has no custody. Again, contact when it occurs may be restricted to special occasions.

The parent with custody, usually the mother, tends to resent this pattern, seeing the other parent as one who offers treats when it suits him. However, fathers talking of their experience in Burgoyne and Clark's book, *Making a Go of It*, felt that their presence was resented by stepfathers. Possibly it is disliked by mothers too, because of their desire to produce a new, cohesive family unit. Fathers are a reminder of an unhappy past (no doubt all this applies in reverse in the few cases where mothers are non-custodial).

The father who offers treats is often unpopular with his ex-wife, especially if she is struggling to make ends meet, though offering treats may be the only way he can demonstrate his caring. The underlying dislike is because it is not only seemingly a bribe, it is also an indication of lack of intimacy and a need to entertain a child rather than be with him or her in an easy, taken-for-granted manner. But it is difficult to avoid such a problem when visits are brief or spaced out, and joint custody, or at least a regular pattern of living together, puts a very different complexion on 'treats'.

Harriet's ex-husband, now living just round the corner from the old family home, can combine treats with daily routine, says Harriet. 'We have joint custody and our son goes there every weekend and has his own room there. They go out together every weekend and they have a high old time. Now this is against the rules, isn't it? Mum is the one who spanks you and puts you to bed and forces you to eat, and Dad is the one who takes you to a hotel for a slap-up lunch and swimming—and I don't give a damn. If my son has a nice time, why worry about it? He sees his father in his terrible state sometimes, drunk or whatever, and that's much more sensible. They have a proper relationship.'

Ian, the teacher, who gave in to his ex-wife's demands in order to have reasonable access to his children, now has them with him every weekend and in the holidays. 'I suppose you could say I do take them for outings, but they are things we really enjoy doing together, like going to the cinema. And then they also do things with me at home. My daughter likes to cook, for instance, and we often do it together, and my son recently decided to paint a cupboard. He didn't do it very well, but I was pleased he offered. It meant that he wanted to do something for the home.'

Ian's ex-wife now lives with a new partner who is unmarried. Ian sees this as a reason why he has the children more often than he used to. 'They have no children between them, and it's clear she doesn't want any more. I think they are in the way, and now she's only too happy to get rid of them. She has become very career-minded too, and her work is taking up a lot of her time.'

This suits Ian, who is a devoted father, but he is also angry. 'I object to the way she neglects the children. I think it is extremely bad for them to feel unwanted, and I do my best to make up for it.' In other words, being a devoted father can be a way of getting back at an ex-wife, a point which has not in fact escaped Ian. 'Of course, it is easy to feel superior when I have long school holidays and she doesn't. And I do see that she needs time with her new man—I'm not that ungenerous. But the anger does come out when you feel you are being used. The best thing about it is that it is a flexible situation. When there are two family homes, it's easy to get away as a couple at weekends because the children have somewhere else to go. And if you have a child who you are not getting on well with, they can go and live with the other parent. That's not an option you get with the ordinary nuclear family.'

The troublesome adolescent who moves in with dad—the most usual route when there is parent-child friction—may indeed feel she or he has extra options. The one danger is that there can be an element of punishment and rejection in the air, along with a 'let's see him try to handle it' attitude to the ex-partner.

Fathers like Ian, who are prepared to increase time with their children, are in the minority. Our ordinary pattern of family life, with mother looking after the children and father out earning money to support them, makes it easy for men to remain fairly distant and to relinquish their children with less anguish than women customarily do. Against that must be set the fact that men may have been driven out by close-knit mother-child bonding, especially if the marriage itself is unsatisfactory. Or of course the easy breaking of links now may reflect an initial low commitment to fatherhood, which may well have contributed to the break-up of the marriage. Many men only come to realise the importance of their children after they have left them, and then use this to strike out at their ex-wives by claiming they are unfit to be mothers.

Marianne Takas, in *Ms* magazine, lists the publication of a steady stream of divorce books for men which advise on ways to win custody, such as accusing women of lesbianism as a bargaining technique. Father-love may not always be the true motive. Takas claims that one in three men in America use the threat of a custody battle in financial bargaining during divorce. As Christopher Clulow points out (in chapter 2), British men, too, use this device.

For men who miss their children, the problem might be solved by pouring love onto stepchildren or a child of a new union, a solution which an ex-wife will note with cynicism, remembering years of neglect.

This is possibly how Norman's ex-wife might feel. He himself admits that he hardly knew his son, who was three when he separated. 'I was busy building up my career, and that meant spending over a third of the year out of the country. Now with Peter [his son, aged five months, from his second marriage] every moment with him is precious to me. I think about what he will do when he is older, what he will think of us, whether he will like where we live. I find myself talking to him, holding conversations I hope we will have in the future.'

To some extent, Norman's son in this second marriage is having to make up for the floundering relationship Norman has with his other children, both of whom show distress when visiting. Norman feels similarly distressed, acknowledging that the children cause disruption in his new family unit. 'We ask ourselves, and we can justify doing so, do we want the intrusion, do they need the disturbance? People like the Stepfamily Association say that the disturbance at the moment is something they should suffer, or else they will regret it in the long term.' And that goes for Norman too. It is as difficult for men to admit to themselves that they would rather not see their children as it is for women to admit that they have chosen a new partner despite their children's lack of enthusiasm.

Norman feels that his children lack discipline and have deteriorated in behaviour since he left. 'They know the rules. They always asked to leave the table when I was there. They've unlearned it, and now they have to learn again. My daughter has also learned that there is no point in sulking. At home she's been allowed to get away with it. On holiday she was told quite forcibly that if she wanted to sulk she could do it on her own because we didn't want to be affected by it. And she hasn't really sulked since.'

But she cries instead, when she visits and when she leaves, and perhaps cannot understand that Norman's anger towards his ex-wife and towards himself is overflowing onto her, and that his insistence on rules is to keep things under control.

Now his ex-wife has remarried, and he says he has no views on this. 'I will be able to voice my views when I see the man over a period of time, and see how the children react. At the moment my son tells us that his stepfather doesn't play with him at all. He just comes in and sits down in front of the telly. Well, he is a long-distance lorry driver and that's all he might want to do. I talked to my former wife about this and she says he does do things with the children like go out and wash the car. So my son could be telling me something that I want to hear . . . And when my daughter comes here and says her stepfather has told her off, I won't jump immediately to her defence because I want to know from her why he has told her off. It's difficult for her to take, but she has to learn.'

Well, it's one way to tie oneself up in knots! It would solve many problems if Norman's children settled well with their new stepfather, but when you are also a rival for their affections, and you feel anger towards a child and have a need to teach her a lesson, you don't necessarily choose the most obviously favourable path.

Graham's current situation with his children is the one the Stepfamily Association predicts when there are no visits, and no disturbance. The children were aged seven and ten when Graham's first wife asked him to leave. Having been made redundant at about the same time, as reported earlier, he went to Canada to start a new life. Margie accompanied him there with her three young children, but then decided to return to England after a few weeks, and Graham quickly followed. 'When I came back I said to my ex-wife, "Can I see the kids sometimes?" and she said, "They couldn't stand the shock of hearing you'd just come back, so you must write first." I thought that was bizarre.' Unfortunately, from his wife's point of view it may not have seemed so bizarre to punish a man who was prepared to put 3,000 miles between himself and his children, even with extenuating circumstances.

Like Norman, and like many young husbands trying to set themselves up in work, Graham had given little time to his children, and the habit of making work the priority had stuck. He describes his job before redundancy as all-absorbing, taking him away from home three days a week.

Leaving home for good emphasised his very slender tie with his children.

Graham's ex-wife's attitude was another important factor. Inevitably there is now great emotional distance between father and sons, a development Margie regards with regret. 'We don't know how his children feel about us now. They are fifteen and eighteen and we know nothing about them really. Their mother put a lot of blocks in the way in those early years when it is important to maintain some kind of ongoing relationship with the children. They were more of a threat to us than my kids, very manipulative in many ways, even though they didn't live with us. They've been to child guidance and the older one is in trouble with the law. But we tried. I've wanted to be friendly, but they don't answer. You know, I could shake them sometimes. It's a shame.'

Graham recalls the strain of trying to remain in touch: 'I would say we worked hard fairly consistently for the first three or four years, but I know that when I saw my kids every week, every Friday was "Ugh day", you know? Because it was so tense. In the early days I felt guilty. It took me days to recover, and then I began to get tense a couple of days before I saw them again. I don't ask about home life any more because it gets boring. There's no conversation, you don't get an answer, and that's the strain. You've got nothing to say to them.'

What this means is that there is too much to say, most of it unacceptable. Graham considers that his sons have had a 'dreadful upbringing', that their mother is a rigid disciplinarian who at the same time provides them with little warmth and no comfortable home life. His sons seem to take their cue from their mother, who perhaps felt neglected or frustrated before coming to the point of telling her husband she wanted him to leave. There may be jealousy on the part of the ex-wife and the sons over Graham's new happy life with Margie and her children. Only where finances are concerned is there no conflict, since Graham gave his ex-wife the house and an agreed lump sum on divorce, and still pays maintenance for his younger child—an example of an amicable arrangement early on which created no space for harbouring resentment.

Graham has come to terms with his family situation in two

ways. 'I tried to be realistic and resigned myself to the fact that I hadn't actually liked my children very much. I love them I suppose because they are part of me, but I can't recognise that. I don't recognise me in them, and I don't think they are particularly nice. I get on with Margie's children better than I get on with my own. Hers are nice kids and they have been accepting more or less from the word go.'

Margie disputes this last point, recalling mutual hatred between Graham and her daughter, then twelve. But Graham brushes her reminder aside: 'It was difficult for her. I didn't have any reason to hate her.' On the contrary, Graham has become what has been termed a 'sociological father' and he has every reason to make himself an important part of his new family and to blot out the guilt and the failures of his old one.

Margie's ex-husband has made it easy for Graham by visiting the children less and less frequently. Says Margie, 'First it was once a week, then once a fortnight gradually phasing out to once a month and then really very little the last couple of years. I think he realises he's losing things though. It came out the other day that David, my youngest, would like to see more of his dad, although he looks upon Graham as his everyday dad, which I thought was a rather lovely way of saying it. They have a terrific relationship. Graham's the one who always comes to the school meetings with me. That's something he never gets with his own boys. But if anything happened to my children, the first person I'd talk to would be their dad. And I do see David still needs his real dad.'

But Graham in some ways is uncertain about visits from the father. 'It's difficult for me because I appreciate how David feels, but I couldn't take too much more of Margie's ex coming into our life. David gets so uptight after the visits.'

This startlingly ungenerous view in the light of his own experiences may be inspired by a preoccupation about Margie's ex rather than David's dad. Margie suggests that the tension partly arises because David sees his father so rarely. There could be many reasons—torn loyalties, unexpressed anger, guilt, or simply the unsaid protestations of love. The reasons apply to father as well as son, and time is needed for them to emerge.

Jim, now aged thirty-nine, and remarried with a second family, was in his early twenties when he left his first marriage. There were two children who stayed with their mother, aged two and three. 'My first wife soon got involved with someone else and then they got married. Next thing I got were adoption papers. They didn't want me to see the children at all. The social workers advised that the kids would go through hell if I opposed it. The husband's argument was "I don't want this Father Christmas figure coming round. I'm the father, and that's it." The social workers said one day the kids would look me up again. And that happened. Now they are sixteen and seventeen, and they first looked me up a couple of years ago. They come round once a month and our two boys really love them.'

Steven inherited Sandra's two sons and was not hindered by their biological father who maintained little contact. Steven's own sons stayed at weekends, and the four boys got on well. Now Steven's boys are in their late teens and Sandra's in their early twenties.

Looking back, Steven considers that discipline was the biggest problem in his second marriage. 'Let's say 80% of the arguments have been over the children, with my ex-wife causing the other 20% . . . I wouldn't honestly say I coped very well. Sandra's oldest is not very verbal, more a physical type, and there was a lot of umbrage between us at first. The younger, funnily enough, has modelled himself on me and is into wine and things like that, which I wouldn't have expected. But though there were scenes, the fact that the boys got on made it easy. There was no sibling rivalry. One of mine would pair off with one of Sandra's, and though she felt mine were less house-trained than hers, she treated them all alike. Hers had their lapses so it balanced itself out in the end.'

Having the children in harmony is obviously a great advantage. Says Sandra, 'We've had lots of disputes over the boys, none insurmountable, though they ate huge amounts of food, caused loads of washing, and wore me out in many respects. One of the things we had to come to terms with was that we had no children between us. But my eldest son has two small babies, and that has been a substitute for us. The grandchildren are our shared grandchildren. That's how it seems to us.'

John, too, found himself bringing up a young stepson. He married for the first time at the age of thirty-seven, and taking on Milly's two children, then six and eight, was a brave task for a bachelor. 'It was leaping in at the deep end. Here was I, a child of divorced parents, trying to deal with a very disturbed boy of eight who had got used to playing the male role with his mother.'

John is a librarian, and found common ground with his small stepdaughter, who was academic, but not with his stepson who was very active physically, and not at all verbally expressive. 'Simon was very attached to his father, and saw him once a week. He resented me. It was a question of us being two male rivals for their mother, and I actually learned a lot from him. I once or twice tried clouting him and that didn't work. Gradually I saw that he was someone you couldn't dragoon into anything, and as he got bigger he was more difficult to control.'

Milly wanted to make it clear that she had never hit her children. 'But I felt that perhaps I was wrong, and he needed firmer treatment.' This uncertainty could have led to disaster, with the child playing up and exploiting the situation. But both John and Milly were sufficiently flexible and trusting in this case, which meant that such a development was avoided.

John soon found his disciplinarian approach inappropriate, but appreciated the way he was allowed the freedom to try it. 'When Simon and I had a row, Milly let us get on with it. She said it was no good her intervening because we had to make the relationship and she couldn't dictate how it should be. That was very healthy, and we managed over the years. Getting people to do it themselves is hard but necessary.'

This description fits very well with Papernow's theory: by stage 5, Action, the stepparent and child are able to work things out between them, with the natural parent taking a back seat. As in Steven's family, stepfather and son had formed a strong bond between them. Says Milly, 'The funny thing now is that they have a fantastic relationship. I love the way Simon gives John advice. He has more differences now with his own father. Both the children do care for their father and feel responsible for him, because they understand now why the marriage ended. [It was due to the father's mental illness.] But it is a duty in a way. I'm not sure about love any more. They have after all grown up with John. It has been nineteen years, and though there was no question about who was their father, they got to an age when they could see who they related to most easily.'

In chapter 6, it will be seen that Milly remained in steady contact with her ex-husband, and gave her children every opportunity to keep a relationship with him alive, with full support from John. Perhaps this enabled the children to make their choices without guilt or pressure, despite the unhappy start.

It is, of course, time that takes the difficulties out of the stepparent/stepchild relationship. The experience of living together, of gaining trust and intimacy, provide the proof of goodwill. Gradually, with maturity, a child can learn to make choices without rejecting and with love. If this happens, it is a good lesson in life. One of the reasons that the nuclear family evolved was in order to avoid choice, but that simple family structure is breaking down because choice is something we increasingly demand. We have to learn to live with our choices in more creative and less destructive ways.

Chapter 6
EX-COMMUNICATION

The division between the sexes is never more apparent than in relations after divorce. Tales of injustices have a depressingly stereotypical ring. If *he* is ruthless, treacherous and selfish, an utter bastard, *she* is neurotic, disturbed and calculating, the bitch. Men have the financial power, women the manipulative edge. No wonder the best that most ex-couples can manage is a fairly cool indifference easily pierced by a rather low-threshold tolerance.

Sometimes there are good reasons for bad feelings. A non-custodial father who never visits his children and offers no maintenance when he can clearly afford to do so is likely to inspire understandable bitterness in his ex-wife. If her new partner is impoverished through his maintenance payments to his ex-wife and is denied access to the children as well, there will be further cause for animosity. Of course working second wives object to stay-at-home first wives; first husbands who have given up their property in divorce settlement object to lovers or second husbands moving in. But sometimes it's possible to see the other side of the story . . . the ex-wife who is still too thrown by the divorce to go out and get a job, even supposing she has suitable qualifications; the woman who has a new lover move in (perhaps made homeless by his own divorce settlement) rather than moving out and risking losing her home and that of her children. The hidden message that it's All Their Fault doesn't always hold up.

Recrimination may be irresistible for some people and may even serve a useful purpose for a while. The need to go over old wounds and reassess them, sometimes initially with extreme indignation and a sense of outrage, is part of the separating process, the emotional divorce. We do have to relive our past in order to make sense of it.

But it is very easy to get stuck. Instead of coming to terms with the past and giving up the luxury of harbouring grudges, an ex-partner can take on the permanent role of scapegoat, a role with great potential. If things aren't going too well with the children, ganging up with the new partner against the old offers a superficial solution and avoids criticism of current affairs at home. Self-examination goes by the board when you have a convenient alternative.

There is little to encourage people to achieve a sound basis for co-existence after divorce. Therapists and counsellors make a big thing about 'letting go'. Failure to do this, they say, will prevent a new relationship from forming and may damage an existing one. In practice it tends to mean reducing contact to the very minumum. Friendship between an ex-couple is seen as a kind of incest, as if it must include 'wife-swapping', multiple sex or other non-family activities.

Certainly, letting go is an essential part of any changing relationship. But not much thought is given to how ex-partners might relate beyond a diplomatic cease-fire, or how the policy of letting go can work best, given the very important fact that children are known to benefit from high contact with a non-custodial parent.

Researchers are beginning to say that divorce should be seen as a transition in relationships rather than a dissolution, something that changes with time. The evidence is that it tends to stay the same in that people continue to harbour old grievances. Californian psychologist Judith Wallerstein found that anger was the most intense emotion felt by 40% of women and 30% of men in over 100 divorced families she had surveyed. Some were still intensely angry as long as ten years after the divorce. On average, it took women three years and men two years to regain stability and a sense of proportion. During that time parents were less attentive to their children and were more likely to show anger and to view the child as an economic burden or the symbol of a failed marriage. Clearly such a state of affairs demands a new approach to the way divorces are handled, and there is increasing interest in conciliatory services and the role that family courts might in future play—more on this in chapter 10.

According to various reports from America, a certain pattern of behaviour between couples after divorce is known: women are less prepared to retain contact than men, except when they have left the children with their father; couples without children break away more quickly than those with; reasons for meeting are to discuss legal problems, division of property and the children; women, more often than men, agree to make contact through the instigation and persuasion of mutual friends.

Most of this is common sense. Children are the main reason for maintaining contact with an ex-partner, so it is more likely that fathers will make the running, since they are in the majority as non-custodial parents. Women may fear contact because they feel they will come out worse in any argument or legal wrangle (not necessarily true in reality). And women tend to have a better social network and support system after divorce, so they may find it easier to let go, though they are also more open to the intervention and persuasion of friends.

A study of 118 newly separated people, followed up over a period of thirty months by Bernard Bloom and Konnie Kindle of the University of Colorado, showed that time did not improve the quality of the relationships, which were mainly defined as extremely stable, but in the fair to poor category. Least frequent contact was noted between couples where the duration of the marriage was under five years or over fifteen, perhaps because there may be fewer children in shorter marriages, and in longer ones children are older and less dependent on parents for making contact.

Since one in four marriages in England and Wales ends before their fifteenth anniversary, and fourteen out of every thousand children under the age of sixteen experience the divorce of their parents, there are a lot of parents who might be trying to maintain contact and let go at the same time, while achieving a relationship in no more than a stable fair-to-poor category.

However, research from Sweden, comparing two groups of divorced couples (493 cases in 1971 and 1482 cases in 1978), indicates that relations between ex-spouses can actually change and grow. About one third of the women in both samples, including those who had remarried, claimed that their current relationship with their ex-spouse was better than it had been during the marriage. About one quarter of the remarried men came to the same conclusion, while even more of the unmarried men did so (44% from the 1971 sample, 35% from the later one). Men reported more contact with the ex-spouse than women did, no doubt again mainly because of the children, and in the long run, remarrieds were more positive about their ex-spouses than those remaining single.

Meanwhile, American psychologist, W. Glenn Clingempeel, looking at what he called 'quasi-kin' contact, found that there was 'higher marital quality among those who maintained moderate frequencies of contact' with an ex-spouse compared to those displaying high or low contact. He adds a cautious and possibly narrow-visioned note: 'Very open and permeable boundaries . . . may bombard the remarried couple with role ambiguities and thus prevent the development of some minimal level of marital cohesion.' But the message is clear: high contact with a non-custodial parent is good for the kids (as shown earlier in this book), and moderate contact is good for the grown-ups too.

TRANSITION COURSE

Inevitably, remarriage introduces a new load of complications to add to those already existing between an ex-married couple. Arrangements that have been made concerning the children may have to be rearranged, legal and financial agreements may change, a move of home which could affect access is quite on the cards.

Non-custodial parents may feel jealous, insecure, excluded, curious when an ex-spouse remarries. They may try to extract information about the new partner and about plans for the wedding etc. from the children, who will find themselves in that tantalising position of being able to mislead and exploit for their own sadly dubious ends.

The remarrying partner may be happier, but dreading confrontations, torn about moving home, perhaps guilty and worried about the effect on the children and even on the ex-partner.

Old wounds may open, arguments about money and maintenance are resumed. The fragile strands of co-existence are having to be unwound and carefully woven into an acceptable pattern again.

One of the big problems for ex-couples is that there are no proper guidelines. Widespread remarriage in Western society through divorce, not death, is a comparatively new phenomenon. The game is still being played without clear rules. The 'ideal' of one marriage per person, at least until the death of a partner, has made it easy to ignore the realities of remarriage after divorce. Instead, the emphasis and values have been directed at making a second marriage look as much like a first as possible, which means banishing the bits that don't fit and never addressing the pertinent questions that arise.

What, for instance, do you do to inform your ex that you are getting married again? What are the important factors in the decision to move to a new area? What does Clingempeel mean when he talks of 'moderate frequencies of contact'? And do we really know how dire are the effects of 'ambiguous' roles and permeable boundaries? (Clingempeel also refers to 'the Goldilocks effect', i.e. not too little, not too much, but just right, forgetting perhaps that Goldilocks went for the baby bear's share.)

The rough and ready rule of thumb we tend to apply to these questions usually leaves the non-custodial ex out in the cold. As already noted in chapter 2, social arbiters in America pronounce heavily against the presence of an ex-spouse at a second wedding. Lack of common sense and good taste, they say, which is tantamount to saying the same of any public display of friendly relations with an ex-partner. For the majority, the social dilemma wouldn't arise. Friendly relations don't extend that far. Even so, there are children's birthday parties, children's weddings and other family occasions where the ex has to be tolerated or even honoured. Somewhere along the line, common sense and good taste have to make a sharp U turn.

They may not do so soon enough. American psychologist Lillian Messenger talks of many and varied 'rules' made by families trying to co-exist with an ex-partner. At a series of group meetings she ran for couples preparing for remarriage, one non-custodial parent reported how his ex-wife refused to allow him and his partner to visit his child in hospital, despite the fact that both of them maintained a relationship with the child and saw him regularly and frequently. Such a rule is clearly neither common sense nor good taste, and may well be based on the custodial parent's fear that the child's illness or accident might be construed as neglect, thus providing fuel for a change of custody ruling.

Other 'rules' which form a common experience among remarried couples include picking up the children from outside in the street when they have been visiting a non-custodial parent, never speaking to the ex-partner direct, but sending messages through the children, speaking only to the ex-partner, never to his or her new spouse even when that person answers the telephone and keeping a dark secret of any occurrences, incidences or projects that are not the basics necessary for communication.

There are more positive rules too, like inviting the ex-partner in for a cup of tea when the children are brought back, or taking great care to discuss holiday dates in advance so the children can fit in longer visits. Courtesies would include informing of the purchase of a weekend cottage if weekend arrangements with the children are affected, and of course a cardinal rule is meticulous adherence to time-keeping, with adequate notice of change of plans.

Positive rules can be extremely difficult to live up to, especially if people are still going through an emotional divorce long after the legal one is tied up. The 'rewriting' of the marital history, trying to make sense of what went wrong, makes for a turbulent time and involves much self-absorption but not much detachment. Unfortunately, people still working through their emotional divorce may find all sorts of excuses to create negative rules.

These may range from 'it will upset the child' to 'but as a parent, he/she is so unreliable and will never turn up at the appointed time.' Both might be true, but they are not good reasons for depriving a parent and child of visits. Keeping the ex-partner uninformed about things like holiday plans can be excused by comments like, 'If he/she knows there will be a big fuss', or by the fear of inviting envy and sour comments or, far worse, a request for a change in maintenance if the plans show signs of prosperity. But the real reason could be to do with rivalry and competitiveness. People who suspect others of being envious or competitive are often also those things themselves.

Some parents work quite differently, and compensate for their negative feelings by not allowing children to voice any criticism towards the other parent. This may well be derived from a misguided wish to protect and to stem the flow of their own uncharitable comments. But even if they don't join in, they shouldn't stop the children from expressing their problems. A more fruitful approach would be to think through the criticisms and look for acceptable solutions, possibly with the other parent.

All this suggests that the problem of finding good ways to let go is a tricky one, requiring flexibility and great generosity, and an essentially child-centred approach. To acquire this may involve wading through very murky waters. They sometimes have to, for instance, think of second partners .

WHEN SECONDS COME FIRST

In the Talmud there is a warning for divorced men that goes as follows: 'Don't marry a divorced woman during her husband's lifetime, for when a divorced man marries a divorced woman, there are four minds in the bed.' This of course can apply to women too, who often have to share their husband's earnings and attention with a first wife, and may even share something more. When Glynnis Walker surveyed 200 second wives in Canada and America, she found that 25% felt their husbands were at times still married to their first wives. There was a psychological bond that sometimes went further than a concern for the welfare of the children. Nearly 10% of second wives said their husbands had been unfaithful to them with their first wives.

It is easy enough for second wives to see how firsts might try to lure a husband back, perhaps not so easy to acknowledge a 'harem' mentality that some men might have, or something even more unacceptable—the existence of a sexual bond between the pair. This can be deeply upsetting for a second partner, though it is likely to be part of a shared history, a life that was there before and can never be entirely eradicated. Perhaps the hate-relationship that develops between some ex-partners is a form of protection, a kind of incest taboo which makes forbidden that which might otherwise be tempting.

Such denials and compensations can only be bad news, not only for exes but for new partners. Even the possibility of a shared sexual bond is better handled if it is open to discussion between new partners or is at least better understood by society rather than being suspected or dreaded or made into a taboo subject.

Family therapists are familiar with the 'pseudomutual couple' who get all the messages wrong because they assume that troubles are emanating from the ex-partner. A case history described in the book *The Family Life Cycle* illustrates this very well, and incidentally shows the effect upon a second wife of a husband who is still attached to his first.

The case involved a remarried couple with 'no difficulties' except for the fact that their two sets of children fought constantly. Sally, the wife, supported her husband against his ex-wife, who was seen as a 'disturbed person'. She was willing for him to gain custody of his children so that she would raise them with her own. The therapist explained the need for the children to maintain loyalty and a relationship with both parents, and the husband began attempts to improve matters between himself and his ex-wife.

This destroyed the 'cover' of remarried harmony. Sally tried to deter her husband, threatening separation and termination of therapy. Eventually, she confessed to a strong feeling of guilt and insecurity because they had had an affair when he was still with his first wife. Her need to remove the ex-wife from the scene stemmed from the insecurity and fear that he would be lured back. When this came into the open, it was easier for Sally to hold off and let him have a separate relationship with his children, who gradually resolved their conflicts with their stepsiblings, having less jealousy of their own to contend with.

At the same time, the couple learned to cope better with their ex-partners. It emerged that the husband still had a guilty and intense attachment to his ex-wife, triggered by the fact that he had moved out and remarried in a very short time. Sally had depended heavily on him and had left him to deal with the emotional upsets between herself and her ex-husband. The insistence on their 'pseudomutuality' had turned them into victims, huddled together against the vicissitudes of ex-partners and children.

Second marriages that start off in the old matrimonial home of one of the partners are taking on potential problems. There can be resentment from the children who move out with their mother, and of course from the mother herself. Barbara had no choice but to move into the old matrimonial home when she married Gerald because it was tied up with his business. She recalls how at first her stepchildren refused to visit, but worse than that was and still is the refusal of Gerald's ex-wife to let go. 'She bought a house nearby, which wasn't necessary as the children were at boarding school, and when they were home from holiday she was on the phone here two or three times a day. I felt very guilty. I felt I shouldn't be here, I was living in another woman's house, but I clung to the thought that she might remarry or get a job. I've wavered from feeling extremely sad for her and very guilty, to extreme anger.'

Gerald feels that his ex-wife could never be welcomed in the house: 'The history of her living here for fifteen years is too big.' Barbara recalls a time when the ex-wife visited early on: 'I ran into the garden and hid behind a bush while she raged through the house. It's a territorial thing. Had this been a new house I might have been able to have her here, but she had lived here for so many years I felt she could be taking over again—a very primitive feeling. I didn't want her to see the changes I had made. If she had married again it might have been different. With Gerald, well she would try to get him into the bedroom if she could manage.' (Gerald denies this vigorously.)

The couple, their children and their stepchildren are undergoing family therapy at present, and have tried to persuade Gerald's ex-wife to participate, with little success. There are of course some ex-partners who never recover from their bitterness, even when overtures are made, and who continue to be destructive to themselves and to those around them. Perhaps the boundary Gerald chose, excluding his ex-wife from the house, was too harsh, but then he had his new marriage to protect and a need to make a rule that symbolised a clear separation from someone who showed no effort to separate herself.

Second husbands may find first husbands holding on in a different way, using money perhaps to show that they are a force to be reckoned with. One of the challenges for 'sociological fathers' who take on their new wife's children is the biological father who comes in showering gifts and providing treats, especially when things like basic clothing would be more useful. Even if the gifts are genuine love offerings, a compensation for other forms of giving, a stepfather may feel a sense of rivalry if he can't match the gifts himself. Compared to this situation, the absent biological father is a godsend—for the adults of course, not the children.

Here is where a new rule of remarriage would be of great help. If convention decreed that it was bad sense and bad taste for non-custodial parents to lavish inappropriate gifts, the positive mode of conduct would be to get step and biological parents together to work out an agreement. But this constitutes extraordinarily difficult proposition for those who are not yet emotionally detached after the divorce. Almost all financial problems between ex-marrieds are a reflection of their emotional problems.

COPING WITH THE ANGER

Showing anger towards another person can be extremely destructive, which is why people go to great lengths to avoid it. The positive, assertive ways of expressing disapproval involve self-control and self-awareness, which most people find hard to achieve in the heat of the moment. So the anger goes underground or gets diverted. Contrary to accepted belief, sometimes this diverted anger produces acceptable results.

Harriet, who has an amicable relationship with her ex-husband, has poured her anger onto the third party, an obvious and popular target. 'I was trying to think where all the bitterness had been directed, and there is no doubt that it has gone to the person who he had an affair with. She was a friend, and it had happened to her in her first marriage. I don't know what I'd do if I was confronted with her, except spit in her eye. I've rationalised, I think reasonably, that she let me down, because we all know that if you're sitting in a room with somebody else's husband and you've had a few drinks, it's so easy . . . blokes are not terribly restrained, and you have to say no, as simple as that.'

If only it were always so simple. But the odd come-on after a few drinks doesn't have to lead to a full-blown affair or a full-blown divorce for that matter. And why is Harriet not angry with unrestrained blokes, or at least with the one she married? Perhaps it is simply safer and more convenient to be angry with someone distant.

The third party in this triangle removed herself from the scene shortly after the separation, but Harriet has a very clear morality and would never have considered a reconciliation. 'To me fidelity is terribly important, mental and physical, otherwise I can't cope with it. I felt our relationship was ruined. He had spoilt the whole thing. I was virtually left homeless when my parents divorced, when I was sixteen, and when I saw my marriage slipping away and I hadn't got the security I find satisfying, I threw him out.'

Despite this, Harriet's joint custody arrangement with her ex-husband works remarkably well. 'We occasionally have a drink together and talk about our son and how he is getting on at school or whatever. Or I go round to his house and drop something in and we have a drink. I seldom get cross with him. We sit down and work things out like summer holidays. I've given him lots of advice and said for God's sake find yourself someone with no entanglements, no deception. I would be very happy for him to get remarried, and presumably any future wife would not bear me any malice because I would not be ruining her prospects by taking financial support from her household.'

By achieving economic independence, Harriet has found the security she needs. Her achievement also means that she has no need to be angry with herself for having married a man who proved unable to meet her standards. The absent third party in this case is a useful scapegoat.

For Janet, a bit of positive thinking has helped her to make a good relationship with her ex-husband, though she also gained enormous support from her two to three years of psychotherapy as described in an earlier chapter.

'I could if I wanted to say that my ex-husband had been totally selfish and had expected me to be part of his baggage, was physically utterly insensitive and that he is still a cold fish. But it wouldn't get me anywhere and it wouldn't be good for our on-going situation given that he is still the father of my children and I have to see him every week. I sometimes think those things, but it is not the main thread. Even if it is 50% of the thread, I am going to act as if it were 20% of the thread because that's the only way forward. Working out a lot of the anger in therapy allows me to take a broader and more generous view. It would be poisonous to me and the children to take any other.

'I once told a woman I didn't know very well that my ex-husband was clever and generous and kind and civilised, and she laughed and said I'm so glad to hear that. I do hate women who go on about their ex-husbands being absolute bastards. After all, if you say that it only reflects on your poor taste in the first place. There's a gem of truth in that. I think it is more constructive to look back and see what the good things were. If you turn somebody you have spent all those years with into a slag heap, it doesn't leave you with a great deal to go forward on.'

Bob's divorce was conducted with the minimum of acrimony after he drifted out of his marriage and went to live with Sylvia. 'The only time we've crossed swords was when I reduced my payment by about fifty quid a month. That was because I had given her the house, though it's part in trust for the kids, and then I realised that she was earning her own salary and being supported by her new husband as well as me. However, last weekend I was back there and we were all smiles and whatever.

'From time to time at the beginning we would go out together, with the children and Sylvia too. It was necessary then. An effort, damned difficult to do, but when you're actually doing it, it becomes a pleasurable experience. You're all together at the theatre and you pass the chocolates. It's a question of going out of your way to oil the wheels, and the benefits can last for years. The kids can see that everybody gets on. When I go to collect them, we'll always stay to have a cup of tea. It may not be 100% relaxed but it goes on on the surface. There may be tension underneath but superficially it works and there's no unpleasantness.'

This very English manner of doing things has its advantages, though phoney mateyness may not be to everyone's taste. There are dangers too—if you go too far in ignoring tension, you can end up playing a very unreal game in terms of human relationships, and that's no great lesson in living for children to learn.

Nothing beats open enmity for bad lessons in living. Graham copes with the enmity between himself and his ex-wife by refusing to admit that it matters. He says, 'I have come to terms with my first marriage by dismissing it from my mind. I really couldn't care less how she feels and I don't worry or concern myself about her. The irritation she's been for eight years, just trying to keep in contact with the kids, is unforgiveable. We've always had to pick up the kids and bring them here, and she wouldn't even let us into the house. She thinks I have ruined her entire life although I would say the reverse is true. After all, she asked me to go . . . I was extremely angry, and still am. We'd had years of a cold relationship.'

This does not sound at all like a man who has dismissed the subject of his ex-wife from his mind, or who could not care less. But it would need enormous effort to remove the grudges on both sides and reach a state of mutual forgiveness. It is unlikely that Graham and his ex-wife will ever do this. On the face of it there is no incentive to work at an ex-partnership—that is, if one ignores the needs of the children (Graham's elder son had been in court for stabbing one of his classmates. Graham discovered this by chance on the day before the court appearance).

For a couple concerned about their own relationship in remarriage, conciliation with an ex-partner could appear as a threat, which may be one reason why it doesn't happen all that often. Margie, Graham's second wife, has been making efforts with her ex-husband since she discovered that her young son

David wanted to see more of him, but she recognises certain difficulties.

Margie: He does come here a bit, for David's birthday, and I think now he'll come a bit more. But it was difficult for Graham to cope.

Graham: Insecurity, obviously. Having one marriage collapse, of course you're afraid that the second one will do the same, and having an ex around is, well, it's like stags fighting. I'm not really good at defending territory I suppose.

Margie: But you don't have to really, do you?

Graham: It's instinctive. Everybody surely must feel put out when somebody comes into their house and celebrates their children's birthday in preference over them, and they have all the honours and fêting, the cutting the cake and whatever. I forgot to get any film. I must have Freudianly forgotten. I'd feel that would put anyone's nose out of joint, wouldn't you?

Margie: But if you'd had a better relationship with your ex over the years it would have made it easier for you to understand. If you'd been allowed to go in the house and still been reasonably friendly, and she'd accepted me, then it would have been different. I think over the years, the fact that Graham has had such distant contact has made me very curious about her, and the jealousy of her, which I think is a very normal thing that happens—I wanted to see her, what sort of person she was, what sort of home they'd lived in.

The cups of tea and drinks that pass between ex-couples as they sit in each other's kitchens making small talk about the children serve a useful purpose which Margie is denied. Even so, friendship can be a source of insecurity and not only in the way that Graham has expressed. Janet has worked hard to achieve a real friendship with her ex-husband, but she also sees that friendship as a potential threat in certain ways.

'My ex-husband comes to pick up the kids every week, and when he brings them back he might stay for coffee. I try to diminish that because I think that in a way he is still dependent on me for company, not so much in a wifely way but in an intellectual one. That was the high point of our relationship and he still tends to come in and start into some book he has finished reading, and I get all enthusiastic because it sounds interesting.

I am conscious of the fact that I ought not to let it happen too often because it might make Sam feel I am still getting something from my ex-husband that he cannot give me, though I also know that he would be quite willing to acknowledge that he is not so intellectual.'

This suggests that some of Janet's fear is to do with her own possible dependence on her ex-husband for the things that Sam cannot provide. She has no wish to jeopardise her present highly satisfactory relationship in any way, whether the threat is from herself or from Sam.

She notes, with some amusement, 'a sweet thing that happened at Christmas. My ex-husband brought Sam a book, a very suitable one, and Sam was quite affected by it. He went around joking for days that the only decent Christmas present he'd got was from his girlfriend's ex-husband.'

The ambiguity of relationships is always a good subject for jokes, if only to cover discomfort. The fact is, we don't find it easy to respond to ex-couples who remain on good terms, or to be an ex-couple on good terms when we consider how the rest of the world might view us—as Brenda discovered when her first husband was suffering from a terminal illness in hospital. Brenda had left Maurice fifteen years earlier, when her son was just two. She is remarried and has no other children.

'We kept in touch because I did not want my son to forget who his father was, and over the years I found myself more and more responsible for my ex-husband. His mother died, and this upset him dreadfully. Then a few years ago his sister committed suicide, and shortly after he lost his job. He got very depressed —he was living alone—and was given antidepressants. He had no other family by then, and I found myself becoming responsible for him. I would speak to the doctor about his depression and try to keep an eye on him.'

A couple of years ago, Brenda's ex-husband was diagnosed as having cancer. He survived two major operations, and when Brenda realised the end was near, she attempted to get him moved from the general hospital into a hospice. It was then that the problems began. 'The hospice was fairly local, so I could visit and so could my son. They agreed to take Maurice and so had the psychiatrist at the general hospital. But then I spoke on the telephone to a social worker about the move. 'Who exactly are you?' she asked. I explained and she said, 'But he has a son who is next of kin.' I pointed out that my son was seventeen and hardly in a position to make decisions about his father. She made me feel as if I was a scheming woman after my ex-husband's money.'

During Maurice's last days, Brenda, her son and her second husband were constant visitors at the hospital. 'I used to wonder what people thought—what a strange thing it was, the three of us being there. They probably thought something very peculiar was going on.'

Fortunately, the conventional standards that Brenda imposed upon herself were only skin-deep. When her ex-husband died, Brenda arranged the funeral and was able to give her son a dignified farewell to his father.

The next chapter illustrates how friendship or close contact between ex-couples may be based on compassion, genuine love or simple economic necessity.

Chapter 7
THE GOOD DIVORCE

What the following five stories show is a kind of normality that cuts through the fears and insecurities expressed by many remarried couples. They also put to the test some of the attitudes of the 'experts' who see the friendly divorce as something suspect.

AN EXTENDED FAMILY

Though Anne hadn't foreseen that she would fall in love, she had been planning to leave her twenty-three-year-long marriage for some time, and had told her family of her intentions. She would go when the younger child was eighteen. But she met Peter and left a year before that time. She had always assumed she would remain in contact with her husband, even though she was deeply unhappy living with him, and Peter coming on the scene made no difference. Anne was forty when she left and Peter, whom she later married, was twenty—a factor that may have helped in the events that followed.

'My main concern was our relationships, all of our relationships with each other. I had plenty of reasons for feeling resentful and bitter, but you have to put aside so many things that you don't want to put aside. Even financial considerations. At first, my husband didn't really believe that I would not come back, despite all the years in which I'd told him of my intentions. I made enormous efforts to keep in contact and see him a great deal. He eventually said that he thought he had lost me forever, but then discovered he hadn't, and that seemed to make him feel a great deal better. Once he had accepted, all the old tensions between us evaporated.

'I don't know that initially Peter was that keen on me maintaining a good relationship with my first husband. He was afraid I might go back. On one occasion, when I said I wanted to see my first husband to comfort him, Peter said he can come and see us here. I knew absolutely in myself that I wasn't going to go back, but he probably wasn't as secure. Over the first two years when we were living together, I saw myself as a bridge between all these relationships, because at that time my husband wanted me back, and Peter wanted me with him, and my children wanted me for themselves, and I had to be a bridge for all these needs. That was what I wanted.'

One of the things Anne did was to arrange a meeting with her first husband and Peter in a neutral setting. 'We went out and had a meal, the three of us. I wanted to do my best to present people to each other in the best possible way. From that things developed better and better. Perhaps it was partly because of Peter's flexibility, being young. The two men got on very well and we became what I would call a contemporary extended family—my first husband, my second husband, and my children. I tried to be the bridge, and I also left everybody alone at times to sort out their own relationships with each other. I had to let go, not control everybody. We would spend holidays together and eventually we became very close. We felt related. Everyone had accepted their position and we were concerned for each other's welfare in the way that a family is. I must add that it was the goodwill of everybody. I was very lucky. My children were absolutely wonderful, understanding and patient and loving. And when Peter and I married, my first husband was at the reception. I don't think it was easy, but he did come. He had started to make a life of his own, and he'd seen that I wasn't leaving him as a person in his life.'

Nevertheless, things were not easy for Anne or Peter. Anne was a mature student, and Peter was also studying. When they graduated, there was little work available in the area where they lived in the family's country cottage which was the only thing Anne took in the divorce settlement. For a time they were very poor.

'We were sorting out our financial affairs. I knew that if we went through a solicitor he'd be going for the sale of all the property and I didn't want that. So we did our own divorce and sorted out our financial arrangements for the children and made our wills. In lieu of not asking for maintenance for myself or going to court, my husband offered to give me a deed of covenant over a number of years.'

Anne has now been married to Peter for six years. A few months after the wedding, her first husband, a businessman in his early fifties, was made redundant. Ten days after hearing the news he had a heart attack and died. 'It was absolutely appalling. The only good thing was that in a strange way I was very glad that we had got divorced because we were so much happier and truly affectionate, and there wasn't any resentment. So my feelings were genuine, rather than being muddled up with anger. But you can't escape the fact that there is the chance that all the traumatic experiences contributed towards it. There's no way you can know whether it did or didn't, but you have to accept the possibility that it did. Something my son told me the other day that he'd said to a friend of his was that it is possible to make a good divorce and that I had done so. That made me feel I had managed in my own way.'

THE SUPPORTIVE REMARRIAGE

Milly was also a wife who left her husband, in this case after twelve years. There were two children, then aged eleven and five, and though Milly had no special intention to keep in touch, she found herself doing so. The marriage had started going wrong around the time the second child was born. 'It was then that my husband was diagnosed as schizophrenic. We spent a lot of time seeing psychiatrists, and one of them suggested the marriage wasn't right anyway. But it's difficult to judge whether that was because he was ill. I was very attracted to him when we first met, and what we needed was an intense affair for a couple of years. But in the 1950s that didn't happen in my kind of circle. I've always felt guilty about leaving, and still do, though I felt it was better for the children. He would accuse me of infidelity and things like that. There were times when he refused treatment, though in the end he did go into hospital voluntarily.'

Soon after leaving, Milly met John, who at thirty-seven and

three years her senior, was still a bachelor. They have been married for twenty years now. Milly's first husband also remarried at about the same time, to a woman Milly knew. The two couples met several times as the new wife moved into the old marital flat.

John recalls some of the early days coping with the situation: 'He was talking about getting married at the time we were. We would have a long, rational conversation and then he would say of his wife-to-be, she's poisoning me. You couldn't say much, but we were worried about whether we should say something to her about it. She was a nice but fairly simple woman, and we wondered, does she understand him at all? We didn't say anything, and it may have been cowardly, but we were reluctant to play God.'

The marriage lasted only five years, but the relationship between Milly and John and her ex-husband continues. Says John: 'I have always accepted him. He is basically a generous and kind man. I have a certain respect for him. He works solidly, he is a silvercraftsman, a nice character. We never asked him for any money because his salary was fairly modest, and both Milly and I were working. She left him the flat because he needed a home, and she went to work in a hostel where she had living accommodation.'

It can have been no easy thing for a woman to move out with two children and fend for herself without any maintenance or any capital, but Milly survived the experience without bitterness. On the contrary, she found herself in the role of protector of her former husband.

'It was always a big joke, the way he kept seeing us. We moved to the north because of John's teaching job, and the children were too young to travel alone, so he would spend every Christmas with us, three or four days, for eight or nine years. When people would ask, "What are you doing for Christmas?" I used to say, "I shall sit between two husbands." It was a break for him, a holiday. He could talk to us, and it was an opportunity to be with the children.'

The experience wasn't altogether comfortable. Says John, 'It always went off all right for me because it brought back no memories. All I felt was that Christmas can be such a lonely time and he had somewhere to go. But I know Milly was rather relieved when it was over.'

Milly agrees. 'We never went back over our relationship and why it broke up, but when he had his problems and started to talk about his medical difficulties I thought, oh here we go again, dragging down, moaning about things, and I just, well it was a strain. This was happening when his marriage had broken up.'

After some years, Milly and John moved back to the south, and her ex-husband continued to visit, even when the children were not there. Now he has found a new partner and is much more stable. A new pattern is beginning:

Milly: She's been round here with him a couple of times. She saw him going through a bad patch a year ago so she knows he is mentally ill, though he manages his life quite well now. When we met the last time she came over to me and we hugged and kissed each other.

John: Well, why not? We like her and we think she likes us.

Milly: If now, at last, over this period of nineteen, twenty years, because of the way we've been towards each other, the three of us, he can find somebody and make a good relationship, then everything has been worthwhile. She doesn't see us as a formidable trio where she has to break in.

John: And we do have real connections, all four of us. We have connections through the children because they visit him and they talk about us, and they visit us and we talk about them. So if we all know each other and like each other, it really simplifies matters.

UNBREAKABLE BONDS

Sue's first marriage when she was in her teens left almost no impression on her. But her relationship with Nick, her second husband, continued to be immensely important, surviving a passionate affair with another man and then divorce and, in due course, remarriage to someone else. Sue and Nick's marriage lasted just four years, during which time they had a son. Then Sue decided to have a trial separation for reasons which she herself says sound bizarre.

'Nick was trying to write scripts for television and earning money by doing odd jobs, window cleaning, anything. I said I'd take the baby and the car and live with my parents, and he could stay in the flat, just for a year, so he wouldn't have to support us and would have a chance to write. We would still see each other and sleep with each other, and I'd get a job.'

By the end of the year, Sue had got involved with someone else. She moved in with him, despite Nick's entreaties for her to return to the marriage, and relations were strained. 'Had he said in a loving, gentle way that he needed me, I would have gone back, but I felt Don, the man I was living with, needed me more.'

Despite this, Sue and Nick remained in touch. 'He found another partner, but we gradually realised that our love for each other did not fade. It wasn't sexual, but I admired him, I loved his humour. I could talk to him better than to anyone. We just spent hours talking to each other. I respected his opinions more than any other man. I lived with the other man for five years and my relationship with Nick strengthened. He came over to us regularly and he was accepted because there was no way I could give Nick up.'

Sue's life with her new man was stormy and insecure. 'But we did have a great time. He worked the markets and there was plenty of cash. But I knew it wasn't going to last forever. I needed something more stable. My son spent part of the time with us, part with his father or my parents.'

The stability came in the form of Jim, to whom Sue has now been married for thirteen years. There are two sons of the marriage, aged eleven and nine. Her son from the marriage with Nick is now in his twenties.

'During the time that I broke up with the other man, my biggest friend and ally was Nick. When I met Jim, the one person I wanted him to meet was Nick. In fact, Jim still says he felt this man is going to make or break me, she is so influenced by this ex-husband of hers.

'Nick would come round, sometimes he'd bring a girl along, and sometimes it was just the three of us, watching television, sharing a bottle of wine, I honestly do not believe that the two men were jealous of each other. Nick had always said that marriage was constricting and that what mattered was people loving each other. My love for Nick was almost like a brother, or a very special, close friend. I can't explain it. I don't like losing people who once meant so much to me. I still feel that about the other man I lived with. We talk on the phone, though we are not really in contact. Of all the people in the world you know, the ones you've been that close to are the ones you don't want to lose—at least it's like that for me.'

Nick was a welcomed guest at the wedding. 'Of course he came. He couldn't come early, because Jim had set up an electronics shop and Nick was running it. Some people at the wedding, some of Jim's old friends, found me weird. They whispered, God, there's her ex-husband. What's the matter with her? Somebody openly said, Are you queer? That can't be a normal relationship. I used to say, But I find it normal. It's your way that seems so abnormal. How can you never speak to each other again after you've shared so much?'

Jim's version of events fits with everything Sue says. 'Nick and I always got on. I knew he was vetting me from the beginning. He was looking at me with the attitude, was I going to be right for Sue and for their son, rather than I don't want you to come into this. When I was setting up my business, Nick came and worked for me. He said I was supporting Sue and the boy and that was his contribution. I couldn't have had anybody better. He had such devotion to us and he wanted me to be a success because it benefitted Sue.'

There is a tragic ending to this story.

One day Nick brought to Sue and Jim's home a young woman. Perhaps it was jealousy, but Sue felt a presentiment of doom. 'I remember she walked through the door and it was like the tragedy that actually happened. She was an Ophelia. Was I jealous? A trace, like when my son first brought a girl home, a twinge . . . he's got another love. But happy for him too because I didn't like him going home to an empty flat. All his life he'd had spells of deep depression. We used to talk about it and he'd say things like, "Trying suicide was a cry for help, I don't find life all that valuable, I can't get high on the things that other people get high on like holidays." It was always worrying to me.'

Nick lived with his new love for eighteen months. He

returned to the flat one day to find her dead from an overdose of drugs. She was twenty-five. Sue's immediate reaction was to protect Nick. 'Jim brought him over to stay with us for the night, and dealt with the police and everything. Next day he insisted on going back to the flat and Jim went with him, then Jim left for work. He seemed in control. Nobody realised how dangerous the situation was. Since then I've joined the Samaritans and I know that if you've made up your mind to commit suicide you are often better because you have found a solution.'

Later that day, Nick poisoned himself with mercury chloride. He had expected a quick death. When that did not happen, he telephoned for an ambulance and survived seven weeks in hospital. Sue and Jim were at his bedside every day. Jim remembers a moment when it looked as if he might recover. 'He told me how much he regretted what he had done, and we talked about the future.'

After Nick's death, the police gave Sue and Jim a suicide note they had found in the flat, addressed to them. In it, Nick asked them not to grieve, told them he had been determined to die. It was ten years ago and they remember vividly every word.

It was now, for the first time, that Jim began to feel jealous. 'Suddenly, I felt Nick had acquired a saint-like quality. He would be used sometimes as an example, and there was nothing to fight against. Before, if she ever made criticisms or comparisons I could talk things out with Nick. Sometimes he agreed with her but often he didn't, and if there were differences of opinion he would always see my point of view. He would say to her, you've got to leave the man alone and let him get on with it. He could be a great help. Now I've got no one on my side!'

Sue says, 'I think Jim felt that Nick now could never ruin what we had had together. It was safe and secure. Whereas the two of us could go on, and we could even destroy our relationship. He was grieving too, but it's not something that can be shared easily. You get locked in your own grief and can't support one another, and that in the end creates painful memories that can come between you.'

Jim actually feels that the marriage took a very different turn when Nick died. 'There was a complete withdrawal of affection and love from Sue, not only to me but to everyone. It lasted months, a year. I was unable to support her at that time. That was probably selfish of me. In the grieving, well you do feel bitter as well. I felt he needn't have done that to us, and to his son who was living with us. That was a great weight for me. I was his stepfather. He had lost his father. It took a long time for our marriage to take shape again. We carried on together because we didn't want to be with anyone else.'

THE CHILD-CENTRED ARRANGEMENT

Very soon after Gill and Ronnie met, they left their marriages —hers of eighteen years', his of twenty years' duration. Ronnie's ex-wife has remained as bitter as she ever was about the break-up, whereas the end of the marriage and the life that followed was amicable and smooth for Gill.

Gill describes her ex-husband as pleasant, but lazy and unambitious, with very little interest in the world around him beyond an obsession with watching sport on television. 'So when I said I wanted to marry Ronnie, he accepted that and was very pleased when his brother asked him to share his flat, and Ronnie then offered to buy his share of the house.'

From the start Gill, her ex-husband and Ronnie were concerned for the welfare of the only child of the marriage, Robin, who was then ten years old. Ronnie's sons were in their late teens at the time and could make choices of their own.

Says Ronnie, 'When I came in on the scene, Robin was bewildered and couldn't understand why I was kicking his father out of the house. We got together, all four of us, and sat round the table and tried to explain everything, tried to give reasons. I would not have been able to move in without cooperation from Robin or his father. Without them, there would have been no way that I would be with Gill now . . . because I knew Gill had to put her son first—it's more that way for a woman than for a man. A woman has a deeper, stronger feeling than a man has. We spoke, Gill's ex-husband and I, in a way that showed we both felt that Robin should have the best possible life without having too much emotional trauma. We tried to make Robin feel that it was his decision whether or not he stayed. We said he would be able to see his father when he liked. The more you stop a boy from seeing his father, the more dangerous it is for the person who is taking over. At the beginning, Robin's father was here a great deal, but even so he has never been dependent on us.'

Gill remembers the meeting as somewhat harrowing. 'We were all very upset. We said that although we liked each other, we were all fond of each other, we didn't want to be together in the way that Ronnie and I did. We said he'd see a lot of his dad, and from that day to this, my ex-husband is on the phone every night. They see each other at least once a week, because my ex-husband comes here for dinner one night a week. And then Robin sees his father here or sometimes out, at the weekend.

'We've had no formal custody or access arrangements, and incidentally, when the decree nisi was heard, we said to my ex-husband, would you like to come to the hearing, so no one could ever say you did not know what went on. He agreed, so after the decree nisi we went in to see the judge because of access, and we asked my ex in front of him, are you happy with the arrangement? And he said yes, he couldn't look after his son. As far as the judge was concerned, we have never seen a man's face with such an expression when the custody proceedings came up. The three of us were sitting there and the judge said who are you, and I told him and so did the other two. And he said I don't understand.

'We all went out to lunch afterwards. It wasn't exactly a celebration, but we tried to put a good face on it. The way we looked at it was like this. It was an accepted fact that we'd been together for two years. Nothing new had happened, but we'd had to go through the formalities. We agreed that we weren't going to tell Robin on that day what we'd been doing. We'd leave it till a few months later and then mention it casually and say what difference does it make to you? Dad still comes . . . it's only a bit of paper.'

Gill suggests that the part she has played was not entirely for Robin's benefit. 'I would have been very upset if I hadn't seen my ex-husband at all, because I am very fond of him. But love doesn't come into it. We're friends, better now than when I was married to him. And I can say that I've worked hard at it.'

THE SELF-HELP SOCIETY

The set-up in Rosemary's household might be described as a *menage à six*. There is Rosemary, now married four years to Martin. They have a daughter aged three. There are also the teenage son and daughter of Rosemary's twenty-two-year long first marriage. And upstairs, with a bedroom and sitting room of his own is Gordon, ex-husband of Rosemary and father of the teenage children.

According to Rosemary, her first marriage 'ran out of steam' several years before the separation. There had been a brief affair at one point, but when Rosemary left she did so on her own. It happened around six years ago when the children were ten and twelve. Rosemary was forty-one. Her mother was living in the house, and by taking a bedsitter nearby, Rosemary could visit regularly. Soon after, she met Martin, unmarried and ten years her junior, who was also living in a bedsitter. At the time, Rosemary had a full-time clerical job. Gordon was a clerk in a firm of accountants.

Nobody is quite sure who decided that it would be a good idea for Rosemary to move back into the family home with Martin when they got married. Rosemary says, 'Martin and Gordon decided it between themselves. We were decorating my mother's room which we always did when she was on holiday. Martin came round to help Gordon, and they got on quite well. It was then that the idea of building an extension came up. Even if we hadn't moved in, I would never have insisted on Gordon selling the house because the children were here. Of course I didn't really like leaving the children. I used to send him money when I moved out, to help pay for them, because he's never earned a lot.'

Martin says, 'I think I suggested moving here. The way I looked at it was that I'd met Gordon and the marriage had broken up before I came on the scene. I could tell there was no animosity. I'd been living in flats of various sizes for some years, and the only thing Rosemary and I could have afforded was a flat, and I don't like them. You suffer from noisy neighbours. This would be the least upheaval. If I'd felt any jealousy or difficulty I wouldn't have moved in. I paid for the extension. I think it must have been more difficult for Gordon as he's the one who's lost something.'

Gordon says, 'I think it might have been suggested first by Rosemary. But Martin and I got on, and it seemed a good idea for all of us. I couldn't feel animosity towards him. He wasn't the one who caused all the hassle. We've never rowed. I've never had any sexual jealousy. I can't see any point in ending with people clawing each other's eyes out. When people pursue others for money—I can't see the point. You get taken to court for more maintenance, and you argue about a pound a week. When you consider what would have happened if we had split the house—both of us would have had a heavy mortgage . . . This sort of situation? Well, there's nothing to it. It hasn't got spice, has it? Everybody likes to hear the bad news. I think there was bitterness at the time, but in the end you say what the hell. When you accept that you're only here for another twenty, thirty odd years, you can't go around with that kind of animosity.'

Lisa, the eighteen-year-old daughter says, 'This seems so natural to me. One of the best ways of doing it. I remember when Mum went away. I was about twelve. That was the worst thing, though she came here a lot. And then when she said she was getting married again, I hated that. The best moment was when the baby was born. I was old enough to appreciate her and not be jealous or anything like that. I wanted a boy, so did my brother. But it didn't matter. I call Martin Martin and I call Dad Dad. Sometimes the baby used to do that when she started talking, but she's got it all sorted out now. The way things are here, it couldn't be better. It's hard to understand how people break up bitterly and get so cracked and the children only see one parent. I can't understand that. I'd hate to live here only with Dad, especially now Nannie [the grandmother] has gone, and then I'd have to go and see them, because I couldn't see them very often.'

Rosemary and Martin started off with a bedsitting room upstairs till the extension was built. They also had their own small kitchen on the landing. Then Rosemary's mother died, and her room on the ground floor became their sitting room. At this stage, Rosemary took over cooking for the entire household.

'We all eat together. Gordon gives me housekeeping, for him

and the children. We still own the house between us. I subsidise the children a little bit, but I work only on a Saturday now because of the baby. Everything else we split down the middle —decorating and things like that. The children tend to wander in and out. Gordon spends a lot of time on his own. He's very much involved with the church. Sometimes he comes in here and sits and chats. After tea they all wash up together. Martin does the gardening because he likes it. It's a bit of a self-help society really. I tend to rule the roost a bit I think. They all shout at me and tell me to shut up and say I'm absolutely horrible.'

Gordon is fully aware of Rosemary's strength. 'Without her it would all fall apart. She's lucky in some respects, isn't she? There are some jobs I'll never touch in the house, and he'll do them, and *vice versa*. I like living in the house. I do my own washing, and some of the ironing and the kids' washing. If I want to be on my own, I'm on my own. I'm in a funny position, if you think about it. I can hear rows going on and I think to myself no, that's the wrong move Martin, that's the wrong move. I wouldn't say anything though. They're not big rows. You know, differences of opinion. Occasionally I can hear her say to Martin what she used to say to me in a row. I can have a laugh. Occasionally, one of them comes up to talk to me about it.

'In a way now I get on better with Rosemary than I ever did. Because you're friends, there's no aggro. It's the niggling things that used to annoy that I don't have to deal with now. I think he's the same sort as me, fairly easy-going, although he has a much shorter fuse. I take a long while to go on the boil. She's a person of quick fire and tomorrow it will be completely forgotten. It takes a few days for me to cool down. She couldn't understand why I couldn't come down as fast as she could. Perhaps it suits her better with Martin because now and again he really puts his foot down, whereas I didn't.'

There are one or two areas that are not to Gordon's liking. He admits to a certain loneliness. 'I'm much more alone than they are. I go down there when I'm invited. They deserve privacy. I tended to drift away from Rosemary's friends deliberately. When we've been to parties together, well, I've thought I could be an embarrassment because they're not really my friends and if I turn up they are not necessarily wanting to see me. But I don't have many friends. It's not easy to make new ones when you're in your fifties. There are a lot of acquaintances you can have a chat to. I'm heavily involved with the church—maybe too heavily. I suppose I am lonely at times.'

Gordon also admits, a little reluctantly, to some jealousy where Lisa is concerned. 'I feel that Lisa intrudes on them at times, when perhaps they want to be on their own. She's always with them when they are watching television, and I don't think that's right. And it means the baby gets too much attention from her. My son is more of a hermit, like me. I've never said anything about it. She's with them a lot when they are talking, and Martin does argue with her, which is useful to her homework. He has more forthright views about politics than I have, and this stimulates her. But then he can be destructive. He can get away with being more critical than a father can. For her, it's a bit of a love affair with Martin . . . All right, maybe there is a little bit of rivalry there. But it doesn't really matter. It's no worse than any other kind of typical family irritation.'

While these things clearly do not jeopardise the family unit, there is always one possibility that would do so. For the first time in years, Gordon is planning a holiday on his own, or rather with a woman friend.

Rosemary's view of this is non-commital. 'Well, I don't know. He might want to get married, and then we would have to think about having a flat I suppose.'

Gordon is equally cautious. 'If I got married . . . this isn't really suitable for a couple. I am going out with someone, and maybe it will get to that stage. If it does, then that's something else we'll have to worry about. I'm not rushing that one.'

Finally, there are Gordon's parents who live fairly near and are visited regularly by the family. Says Gordon, 'My mother is eighty-four and is still making dresses for the little one, though how she can see to sew . . .'

Sometimes Martin goes with the children to see Rosemary's ex-in-laws when neither of the other adults can manage it. Sometimes they have even joined the family on holiday. The three-year-old calls them Grandma and Grandad and sees them with her mother two or three times a week. 'We are a unit,' says Rosemary, 'and we look after our family.'

MURMURS OF DISAPPROVAL

A personal note must intrude here. I told the stories of Rosemary and Anne and Sue and Milly and Gill and others like them to several people while I was researching for this book. I spoke to therapists, sociologists, marriage guidance counsellors, members of the Stepfamilies Association, people who were qualified to make comments on the life styles I have just reported. Almost without exception, there were dark psychoanalytic mutterings, wise shakings of heads. At a meeting of stepfamilies, someone said of the whole idea of close relations after divorce that it all sounded a bit pathological. We had just been hearing an hour or two of the agonies of poor relations after divorce, including suicide threats, horrendous financial complications, instances of spite and emotional blackmail. Nobody registered the irony.

Of course the concept of 'not letting go' came up very often. Sue hadn't let go, nor had Anne, and Rosemary was the arch-manipulator. Well, yes, yes and yes in some ways. But listen to them, I said. See how they work. Therapists and counsellors and people who seek help through the Stepfamily Association understand all too well the examples that don't work. They don't see the ones that do, and may not always recognise them when they come across them.

It is possible to see Anne and Sue as women who are able to continue to love and to care, not as demanding or immature women who cannot let go. It is also possible to see Milly as a person who remains compassionate and protective, not someone feeling guilty and needing to compensate. Ronnie's self-interest isn't necessarily selfish. It can also be recognised as good for everyone else. And if Rosemary is dominating, why must she been seen as destructive rather than a positive life force?

We may search for signs of weakness in the other characters who play such important parts in the stories here. Have they been hoodwinked, taken over, brain-washed? Or might they be regarded as cooperative, tolerant, flexible and in some cases eminently practical, meeting halfway on the bridges that Anne and people like her provide?

What would any of them make of Clingempeel's warning that 'very open and permeable boundaries . . . may bombard the remarried couple with role ambiguities'? No such problem seems to have plagued them. Each seems to know quite well his or her place. The ex-husbands of Milly or Gill or Rosemary feel no more ambiguity than their present husbands do. And who, but themselves, can say that a 'just right' amount of contact with an ex-partner consists of? If there seems to have been 'too much' attachment between Sue and her ex-husband Nick, it is also quite clear that Jim willingly accepted it and never felt excluded till Nick's death forced Sue to make the final break. If one picks out the 'faults', such as the reactions after Nick's death, or the rivalry and slight isolation of Gordon, are they any worse than other problems of relationships described in this book?

It is difficult to understand the cynicism, distrust and even a sense of distaste that stories of so-called 'civilised divorces' incite. (The phrase is always in inverted commas, a defence against its possible reality.) In *Making A Go Of It*, Jacqueline Bourgoyne and David Clark dismiss the idea of 'joint decision separation as the rhetoric rather than the realisation of "civilised" divorce'. One of the families they interviewed claimed that their divorce was amicable and that present relations after remarriage were fine, but this was not investigated. There seems to be a need to deny the validity of a positive relationship after divorce and remarriage, though sheer common sense suggests that it could mean greater harmony and happiness all round.

One of the major objections put forward concerns the children, who are supposed to be confused and in a terrible mess because they don't know one parent from another. Typical views were expressed by headmasters and headmistresses at an annual conference of the Association of Preparatory Schools. The conference was held several years ago, but the ideas are still common. The head teachers were reported to have condemned civilised (or rather 'civilised') break-ups. One stated, 'In the old days, children were still desperately hurt when parents split up, but at least they knew where they were when either the mother or sometimes the father took on the job of bringing them up.'

Another speaker maintained that the worst examples of modern divorce occur where professional parents marry new partners and still continue to meet socially. Children find it very confusing, it was claimed. There was also the idea from a third speaker that civilised divorces might ease the conscience of the parents but did nothing to ease the hurt of the bewildered children.

These statements are fairly illuminating. The first suggests that it is better to know your parents cannot get on after they have split up than to understand that they can be friends even if they no longer wish to live with one another. The 'ambiguity' of the friendly relationship seems to be too disturbing for this speaker to cope with, despite the fact that for most of our lives we have to live with the knowledge that we may not totally like our bosses, colleagues, friends, lovers, teachers, parents, children, though we may like them a lot now and then, or even for most of the time. Surely such ambiguity is highly suitable for children to learn? They have to learn it every time they are told off by a parent or quarrel with a sibling or fight with their best friend; they may as well learn that adults have to live with the problem too.

The second speaker refers to 'professional' parents, which is perhaps a codeword for 'permissive' or 'trendy' parents who have strange theories which they inflict on their young. Well, some do, but that is no reason to dismiss an exploration into tolerance and mutual forgiveness. It is more difficult to understand the third speaker's idea that civilised divorce might ease the conscience of the parents. She could be meaning that a partner who leaves a marriage feels guilty about it and tries to make amends by hanging on to old bonds. When this is one-sided it often does cause stress to the other person, but it is unlikely to do so when both partners agree to remain as friends. Even if guilt is a motivating factor, why should children feel hurt and bewildered if both parents agree to remain on good terms?

The concern over ambiguous boundaries may be greater in observers than in the people who experience them. What would this speaker have made of Rosemary's daughter, eighteen-year-old Lisa, who said, with admirable simplicity, 'I call Martin Martin and I call Dad Dad,' having lived with both for six years? It hadn't taken long for her three-year-old stepsister to work out who was who either.

Headmistresses and headmasters might be expected to base their statements about children after divorce on their observations and also on research which backs up their claims. In this case they almost certainly had no research to back them. To date, enquiries to the National Children's Bureau, the British Sociological Association, the Social Sciences Database at Essex University, and the National Council for One-Parent Families reveal no specific work on children of friendly divorces. There is no evidence beyond the anecdotal to prove that the head-teachers' views are more accurate than, say, Gordon's who is, after all, Lisa's father. 'I totally disagree that children brought up like ours are confused. It's the adults who think like that who are confused because they can't see how a family like ours can live in harmony.'

Perhaps the resistance to amicably divorced partners lies in our ideas about how couples are supposed to be. Men, for instance, are supposed to be possessive and jealous. We may deplore such sentiments, but when we get the alternative we're not sure how to handle it. Men like Gordon, Martin or Jim are somehow made to seem unmanly. Their attitude is not acceptable and does not conform with what we think of as appropriate male behaviour, i.e. 'No man in his right mind would put up with that'.

Women, on the other hand, are expected to put up with a lot. They are acceptable as victims, either the docile or even the complaining variety. An ex-wife is, ironically, less of a threat when she is bitter, spiteful, jealous, grabbing and either frigid or something of a nymphomaniac than when she is, as Rosemary put it, 'ruling the roost'.

Though the cases recorded here have tended to show that good relations begin through the efforts and will of women, there is no reason to suppose that men cannot make similar bridges. If they do not do so, it may be because women traditionally have been the centre of the emotional life of the family. Many men find it easier not to take the initiative or get too involved unless they are drawn in by the women in their lives. Also, men after divorce tend to have a less adequate support network than women, so that an ex-wife might feel compelled to be protective in the way that Milly and Gill did.

We put great value on the healing powers of communication and yet there seems to be much distrust of it when it occurs between ex-partners. Friendship after divorce is a way of acknowledging that passion has died on both sides but at the same time it is demonstrating the fact that the two people still have things in common—things that may have drawn them to each other in the first place. For some people, this discovery is disturbing, bringing in its wake such questions as: was the divorce really necessary? is the new relationship really so much better? We prefer certainty to such unsettling thoughts, even when the certainty vilifies the ex-partner and causes pain and friction. Certainty is romantic, it suggests a perfect choice.

We are brought up to crave exclusivity, not to grow out of it. If there were less concern about having to make a perfect choice and more about continuity, people who find new partners might learn to look at their perfectly sensible doubts and questions with honesty and directness. They might forgive themselves their own mistakes and then forgive the people who helped them to commit them. Mutual forgiveness, followed by mutual giving, are highly necessary in an imperfect world. One of the paradoxes of human experience is that when we act generously towards someone we have felt angered with, the anger loses its force and may disappear altogether if the other person receives the act of generosity gracefully. We heal ourselves by offering goodwill, as any good Behaviourist would agree—and Christians too for that matter!

Chapter 8
FAMILY REUNIONS

Just as remarried couples function best when there is goodwill between the ex-partners, and children function best when there is high contact with both parents, so remarried families function best when the extended family approves or accepts the new household. A study by Estelle Duberman on the family integration of eighty-eight remarried couples showed that remarried relationships were worst where the extended family was cut off or indifferent, better when the family disapproved but was in contact and best when there was whole-hearted acceptance.

Quite the most important people in the extended family are of course the grandparents, given that there are children from the former mariage. Divorce tends to bring women closer to their parents and other members of their family, and the children and grandparents benefit from this. But the non-custodial grandparents (statistically those who are likely to be parents of the father) may be less fortunate. When a non-custodial parent loses touch with the children, the grandparents may well do so too. This could be because they drift away or because they are made to feel unwelcome, especially when the ex-daughter-in-law remarries or lives with a new partner.

When the in-law grandparents don't disappear, however, they may find themselves in a fairly privileged position as 'emotional intermediaries', providing neutral ground between their warring son and ex-daughter-in-law. This was noted in Pennsylvanian families observed over several years by sociologists Furstenburg and Spanier. In some cases, even when the parent is no longer on the scene, the in-laws may try to make amends by providing social or material support. Furstenburg and Spanier found examples of ex-in-laws taking on the grandchildren to allow the new couple some free time together when a daughter-in-law remarried. Nevertheless, only a third of children in their study saw grandparents on the non-custodial side as much as once or twice a month, whereas four out of ten children saw their 'custodial' grandparents weekly. There was little difference in the pattern when parents cohabited rather than remarried.

Grandparents tend to be slotted into categories by sociologists with remarkable ease. One study listed five common roles: historian, i.e. providing cultural link with past; mentor, offering wisdom; role model, demonstrating family relationship; wizard, meaning storyteller; and nurturer, or 'great parent' widening the support system for children. Other works suggest that a major role for modern grandparents is that of 'fun seeker' giving and getting pleasure without responsibility and keeping well away from moral arbitration. And there is a core of remote but benevolent grandparents who live full and active lives of their own and show little interest in their grandchildren.

The two last categories are entirely predictable and in keeping with social attitudes and practices today. Older people are no longer seen as wise or venerable, but may well be regarded as meddling and out of touch, particularly when they apply their own moral standards to their children and grandchildren. Better, then, to avoid controversy and enjoy the fun. The second category reflects the increasing opportunities for women which bring them back into the workplace when the family is growing up, so that they remain active and independent in the years up to and beyond retirement. They have less need as well as less time to enjoy the pleasures of grandparenting. Early retirement too allows older couples opportunities for travel, exploring new interests, taking an active part in community life, so that the grandparenting role may be low in the scale of priorities. And perhaps another group can be included in this category—the late-divorced or early-widowed grandparent, often the woman, who makes a new life independent of family ties.

From the point of view of the person who is divorced, 'non-responsible' grandparents like these are not quite what the children would seem to need. On the contrary, they would benefit most from those other categories which offer continuity and stability to family life. Single parents are unlikely to appreciate fun-loving grandparents. Going home to mother is still meaningful for a divorced young woman with children and limited means. Kathleen Kiernan, in her long-term study of teenage marriage and marital breakdown among people born in one week in March 1946, found that nearly one third of women divorced by the age of twenty-six were living with their parents, and the majority had at least one child. The grandparents, or more often the grandmothers, in these families may provide highly active support as childminders during the day and babysitters in the evenings.

Remarriage, on the other hand, turns everything on its head again. Grandparents who have given refuge to a daughter and grandchildren may have fewer constraints than others to voice their views when a new partner comes along. The children may want to stay with the grandparents; the grandparents may be only too pleased to keep them. There may be criticisms of the new man and opinions as to whether he is fit to be a stepfather. Cohabiting may be frowned upon. For the grateful daughter —or son in a similar situation—close-knit grandparents can have their vices as well as virtues.

Of course grandparents who haven't provided a refuge can put their oar in too when a divorced son or daughter contemplates a new relationship. Life can be especially painful for a widow or widower who feels the criticism of the parents of their deceased partner, especially when it is directed towards the new partner. When hostilities abound between a divorced couple, in-laws may take sides, defending their own offspring and thus helping to increase the difficulties.

A more innocuous but still irritating pressure for remarrieds is the sense of rivalry that can occur between grandparents and stepgrandparents, with each set vying to give bigger and better gifts and treats instead of concentrating on the needs of the children and their new family unit.

It can be quite difficult to get grandparents to change their style and adapt to a remarriage, and some may well withdraw, feeling hurt and misunderstood when criticised. Little thought is given by couples in a second relationship to the reactions of the older generation. As parents of a divorced child, they may have a huge sense of guilt—irrational, perhaps, but in keeping with the 'psychological responsibility' of upbringing, attributed especially to mothers. They may have difficulty in adjusting to being 'instant' grandparents, especially when they have biological grandchildren on their own. They may fear being neglected or superseded when an ex-son-in-law or daughter-in-law remarries or when the new family has a new baby, or resent the burden of stepparenting placed on their own child. They may be worried about future inheritances and where their money will go, and about who will care for them as they become dependent in old age if their children acquire yet another set of potential dependants.

Some of these anxieties are expressed by 'spoiling' the grandchildren or, alternatively, by withholding financial help, or by showing hostility towards the new partner. When the situation is very fraught there is a case for conducting family therapy over three generations, with grandparents, parents and children.

But sometimes it is not fraught at all, and there are examples where ex-parents-in-law provide genuine support and ex-daughters-in-law reciprocate, where there is generosity and sensitivity from parents who can refrain from criticising present or past arrangements. The experiences of the couples that follow reflect some of the anxieties of grandparents, but also some of the acts of generosity and fairness which help sweep away stereotypes and show how remarriage can create a new kind of extended family cooperation.

PARENTS OF DIVORCE

Sons tend to switch alliances from parents to wife when they marry, and when they divorce can find it difficult to return to the protection of their original family. Perhaps that's one reason why they often remarry more quickly. The moral or material back-up that daughters request is usually forthcoming, but there may be strings attached. Parents who disapproved a match do have the opportunity to say, 'I told you so' when it fails, and some take advantage of it. They may, on the other hand, have a sneaking sympathy towards the son-in-law, much to the consternation of their own child.

For Harriet, her mother's solidarity was necessary, despite

her own fierce independence. 'I had this problem with my mother, of all people. Parents' attitudes are very odd towards divorce. My mother was supportive and said she had seen what was happening, but then she was also supportive to my ex-husband and said I'd been so strict with him about his drinking. She actually invited him and his girlfriend round to her house for dinner. I had to ring her up and say no no, hold on a minute. You're my mother and I expect you to support me whatever I do. If your parents don't support you whatever you do, then you're lost really. They can criticise you themselves, but in public they should support you.'

Perhaps in this case the problem was a matter of timing. No matter how fond in-laws might be of their child's ex-partner, extending invitations to them needs to wait till wounds have healed.

Grandmothers may have experienced their own divorce, which should in theory make them more sympathetic towards the marriage breakdown of their own child. But this doesn't always happen, possibly, as already suggested, because they are involved in making a new and separate life for themselves, possibly because both divorces are seen as a personal failure and add to the distresses the grandparent has to cope with.

Chrissie's mother is an example of the latter. 'My mother had divorced a few years earlier because my father had left her the way my first husband left me. She took her own divorce very badly indeed and was very bitter for many years. I think she felt she was not ready to be a grandmother and she couldn't respond much to the children. Now she is loving. She feels that we are very similar in many ways, and my marriage break-up mirrors her own. She hates him, she absolutely hates my ex-husband because it reflects her own experience.'

Such enthusiasm for 'rubbishing' an ex-son-in-law is not particularly helpful in stabilising the relationship between the divorced couple, and positively unhelpful where the grandchildren are concerned. Chrissie received more help from her father at the time of the break-up, and most from her mother-in-law, to be discussed later. 'My father would say things I didn't particularly want to hear, like stop feeling so sorry for yourself and basic things like I think you didn't have your independent life and you were too fused together. That was really very constructive.'

Gill's mother found it easy to strike a good balance with the new family unit and was fully supportive of the way Gill maintained amicable relations with her first husband. 'My mother was very modern in her outlook. She died before Ronnie and I were married, but she showed my son the way. She would buy the same presents for Ronnie and for my ex-husband. She told my son he would be happy living with us and that he would grow up and leave one day and that I wanted to make a good life of my own.'

Sue recognises that she gave her parents a hard time through her two failed marriages and stormy relationships, but she always had their support. 'They have always been there, totally constant. My mother, who was so conventional, has always stood by me, and my father too. They loved Nick, my second husband, and they love Jim too. I don't think they could ever understand why Nick and I parted but they accepted it and provided a home for me and the baby when I needed it.'

Sons seem to get on with their parents less well than daughters after divorce, not only because they don't ask for support but also perhaps because everyone else expects them to stand on their own feet. When they remarry or get involved with a woman who has both children and 'a past' there is a hint that they are being used.

Jim, Sue's husband, suffered unsympathetic treatment from his widowed father for marrying a woman who was older than him and who had a dubious relationship with her ex-husband. 'It might have been different if my mother had been alive, but she died when I was in my teens. My father wouldn't come to the house. It was partly because Nick was often around, and he'd say, "There she is with her ex-husband all lovey-dovey". He'll send us a Christmas card, but he never includes Nick's son on it; it's just to Sue, me and our boys.'

Gerald found difficulty in getting his parents to accept his two stepchildren, though they were happy about his divorce from his first wife. 'They feel very strong loyalty to their natural grandchildren, and the whole idea of my remarrying a woman with children was less acceptable than if I had married someone alone. So we've struggled some years with the pain of all this, like my parents never remembering to ask how my wife's boys are. We've had to lay it on the line and say some things to awaken them to the fact that they've actually got to think about us as a new unit, not just with my two, but with four children.'

One way Gerald's parents could show their non-acceptance was over money and inheritance. 'The biggest stride we've made with them has just happened. I'm in a family business, and my father has been totally unwilling to accept that I have responsibility for two adolescent stepsons who have no family on their mother's side. We say our four children will be treated the same. Now my father's family is pretty wealthy, but he would not acknowledge that anything he is going to leave would be to the benefit of the two stepgrandchildren. Everything was in trust to his grandchildren, so it couldn't be touched by anyone else. But only today my father made a huge concession. He said, "In view of your larger family . . ." and he is making a very generous gesture. That's taken six years.'

Like Chrissie, Steven has to cope with parents who want to rail against the ex-partner. It wasn't quite what he expected at the beginning, when he left his marriage and his two sons and set up home with Sandra and her sons. 'They were dumb-founded, they showed real middle-class horror when I told them. I gave them a long story of what a wonderful person Sandra was and they met her and from that day onwards it was—well, it was absolutely pathetic. They have had less and less feeling for my ex-wife. They are quite anti her, so that if there was any friction between my children and their mum in the past, I would never tell them. I would deliberately withhold it because they would have gone steaming through the roof about her . . . Maybe she deserves it, but that's not fair and I won't give in to it.' And again not fair to the children either, who have enough to work out without the antipathy of their grand-parents towards one of their parents.

The 'only child' is notorious for having possessive parents, and in traditional families when that child is a son, he is likely to feel all the criticism that parents might make about a daughter-in-law. Rob, divorced twice and about to enter into a third committed relationship, is aware that his mother was a cross for his ex-wives to bear. 'They were both less tolerant than I wanted them to be. I am strong enough not to let my mother interfere, but they resented her. My second wife, for instance, felt resentful when my mother spoiled the grandchildren though they weren't her children but mine from my first marriage. With my new partner I am trying to be honest in describing what my mother is like, so she can appreciate that my mother puts me on a pedestal even though we argue, and doesn't believe anyone is good enough for me. She never wanted me to marry my first wife, but after the second of course she said the first one was better. My daughter from my first marriage often brings over her new little stepbrother to see my mother, and that's made my mother more friendly with my first wife than ever before.'

Perhaps it has taken two marriage failures for Rob to realise that he needs to explain his mother to any new woman, and to show quite clearly where his loyalties lie.

RELATING TO IN-LAWS

Fortunately, in-laws do at times rally round, especially when they see a daughter-in-law stranded through the act of their son. It may be a case of selfish genes—grandparents looking after their own kin, their grandchildren—but daughters-in-law do sometimes receive unexpected support.

Chrissie, returning from abroad with two young children when her husband left her for another woman, found her mother-in-law extremely helpful. 'She felt very hurt and upset. She couldn't understand her own son, and she looked after us when we came back because our house was being let while we were away. The children can do no wrong with her, and she was extremely kind to me, letting me live with her for several months. She can be infuriating because she is so over-indulgent with the children . . . I would say that there is a smidgeon less affection towards me now that I'm remarried, because I suppose I've over-distanced myself from her. I don't need her now, but I needed her terribly at one time, though I've never been that emotionally close to her.'

In Cynthia's case there could be no question of selfish genes since there were no children when her marriage broke up. Instead, it was a case of disappointed parents feeling that somehow they had lost a son and gained a daughter-in-law. Cynthia is now in her sixties, and her first marriage took place in 1945, a time when it was very difficult to find living accommodation. 'The old people, my in-laws, got us a flat next to them in London. They thought the world of me. It was all very difficult because when the marriage broke up I left the flat and I also changed jobs because I wanted to make a clean break. Then out of the blue, old Pa found me—something I must have said gave him a clue about where I would be working. By this time I had my own little bedsitter. Anyway, all their sympathies were for me, and every week they used to take me to Lyons Corner House or a show, and it was very nice.'

By 1955, Cynthia had met and married her second husband. 'I introduced them to him, and then we all used to go out, the four of us. My own parents had split up when I was a child, and I saw little of my father. My second husband's mother, a widow, was a strict Catholic and would never accept me. When my ex-in-laws got very elderly, we used to go over there to see them and take them out. Then the old man died, and the old lady was very poorly, and we'd go over. And the funny thing is that the old man left my son from my second marriage some money, not much, but I thought that was absolutely lovely. Obviously, when my son was born they were delighted, and they adored him. He called them grandma and grandpa. They didn't like their son very much. He was not kind to them. When his mother died he did not come down to London for the funeral and he just told a neighbour to get rid of everything in the flat. He was an only child with no children.'

Harriet found that her ex-mother-in-law played an active part in the smooth ending of her marriage and continuing relations with her ex-husband. 'She spoils my son rotten and he is very happy with her. She comes up from Wales in the school holidays and has my son round at my ex-husband's house so I can get on with my work. That has greatly eased matters. I don't like her one hundred per cent, but she is very kind. If you are daggers drawn that kind of cooperation is impossible. I do think people make things difficult for themselves. You have to clear the ground and then say let's concentrate on getting it right.'

Working at a good relationship with ex-in-laws is probably an unfamiliar idea to most people, but it goes with working at a good relationship with the ex-partner too. The ties are strong and need to be acknowledged.

In Margie's case they are acknowledged by her but not by her in-laws. 'My ex-father-in-law is a bit stiff and awkward, but my ex-mother-in-law is quite warm. I think the whole thing, their son going the way he did, knocked them for six. I think they missed me and the children but were not able to show it. They don't come forward. It has to be me. I invite them here for Christmas for a drink, that sort of thing, which perhaps made life awkward for Graham in the early years.'

Graham agrees: 'They were negative at first towards me. It took a couple of years for that to wear off.'

Now, Margie feels that Graham is accepted, 'but perhaps they found it difficult that I could so quickly go into a new relationship.' Graham's parents however were less forgiving. 'They called me a hanger-on with a handicapped child, saying it was ridiculous for him to get involved with someone like me.'

It was not an easy thing for Graham to live with. 'They said Margie was looking for a meal ticket. I think they have accepted her now, but they haven't really taken on her children as new grandchildren. It's partly their age—they are quite elderly. Margie's mum has taken me on very well.'

Money is a very powerful way of showing acceptance, as Gerald has already recorded. When it is the in-laws or the ex-in-laws who have the money, there is more room still for generous gestures, and ungenerous ones. In Cynthia's case, the small sum left by her ex-father-in-law to her son from her second marriage expresses a large amount of love. Janet's story is a less happy one:

'After the divorce I got a mortgage but there wasn't enough money from the family house to buy anything in a reasonable neighbourhood, so I wrote to my ex-husband and said I have to find about another £5000. It happened that his father had died and an unexpected sum had turned up, so the grandmother said it could be used but she wouldn't let it be expressed as my money. She would only let it be used to buy the house if it was expressed in the deeds as a gift from her to the children. At the time I found it very hurtful. It was like saying you will be handcuffed to them to bring them up but you are not fit to be given this legacy. I suppose that was because I had left the marriage. That's the kind of punishing thing you can get with money. The lawyers didn't like it because in a way it creates a divisive interest in the house between me and the children. When the youngest is eighteen they could actually force me to sell up my portion of the house.'

Daughters-in-law, and ex-daughters-in-law, have their own potential power which develops when the older generation becomes frail and dependent. Will Margie be able to care for Graham's parents with goodwill the way Cynthia did for her ex-in-laws? Or Janet?

Gerald's wife Barbara admits to a change of feelings when she heard that at last her father-in-law had recognised her children in his will. 'Gerald's parents are in their seventies and he has only one sister who lives in America, so we are the only immediate younger generation at hand, and I must admit that I was feeling increasingly angry that the burden of looking after them as they get older was going to come my way when I felt I wasn't accepted. I still would have done it, but I do feel different about it now. I know I will do it lovingly and willingly.'

And the most warming story of all must be that of Rosemary, living in her *menage à six* as described in the previous chapter. Her ex-husband's parents, in their eighties, are visited twice a week by Rosemary and the grandchildren. Her second husband is accepted by the old couple, and the child of that marriage embraced as a grandchild. There is also the elderly aunt of Rosemary's ex-husband who is looked after and protected by this extraordinary and yet so ordinary family. There is no money at stake, but ties of history that count more than ties of blood. The lines are blurred, the official relationships made irrelevant by generosity and flexibility and love.

*

THE WIDER NETWORK

There are certain occasions that stir a sense of dread in some remarried couples. Christmas can be one of them, so can birthdays and family weddings, funerals and any other social gathering that could bring divorced people face to face or create a choice about who should be invited or excluded and how the celebration should be shared. Obviously, divorced couples who remain friends or develop a good relationship don't have a problem, except of course when they find that others around them disapprove.

Social occasions with potential problems can be divided into several categories. There are the private ones, like Christmas and birthdays, and the public ones, like weddings and funerals, school prize-givings and parties. Some are centred on the immediate family and most especially the children, some are mainly to do with the divorced couple and the new partner.

On the whole, the private ones settle into a predictable pattern, though not necessarily without friction to start with. There will be trial and error, some irksome fetching and carrying of the children, the inevitable competitiveness rearing its head now and then. But Christmas and birthdays acquire a certain ritual, often with the non-custodial parent getting the children on Boxing Day or switching the festival days each year so that everything is as even-handed as it can be given the circumstances. Birthday parties may include a non-custodial parent being invited in to share in the celebration or at least to have a drink. And even the most estranged parents can usually bring themselves to tolerate a telephone call between the non-custodial one and the birthday child—though surely the best present would be to see the parents making their peace.

It is the public occasion that gives rise to real dilemmas in those doing the inviting and those thinking about accepting. Should both parents turn up to the prize-giving and sit separately, possibly accompanied by new partners? Should a re-married couple attend a party knowing that an ex-partner will also be there? Should the host invite both and also inform both?

Some of the doubts are due to the ambiguity of remarried life. There it is, a commonplace for all to see and many to experience, yet it still tries to slot into place as an original first-time marriage as if all those untidy complications of ex-partners and stepfamilies did not exist. That's one reason to banish a non-custodial parent from prize-givings or a couple from a party.

The divorced and remarried may be guided less by good form and etiquette than by competition and anger. A man or woman with a new partner may be sensitive to the thought of the ex-partner's criticism, which may well stimulate personal doubts too. Those who don't have a new partner to expose to criticism can feel equally vulnerable. They may feel anger towards the person who 'stole' their husband or wife away. And since public occasions are supposed to bring out the best behaviour, hostility will have to be expressed covertly, bringing a sense of discomfort and unrest to the occasion.

Competitiveness in some families may take precedence over the interests of the children. A good example of this is the barmitzvah ceremony that takes place when a Jewish boy reaches the age of thirteen. It is one of the few public occasions which focuses on a child on his own. There is a religious ceremony in the synagogue and customarily a party the following day to which members of the extended family and friends are invited. The synagogue service can accommodate both parents and stepparents. Usually, the biological father will take an active part in this while a stepfather will literally take a back seat.

The trouble begins with the invitations for the party afterwards. If the stepfather is footing the bill or contributing to it, he will almost certainly want his name on the invitations. The ex-husband's response to this will depend on the degree of goodwill between them. The boy's mother may feel very strongly about not inviting her ex-husband or his family. It could and has been known to end up with two separate parties for the thirteen-year-old. One can hardly bear to contemplate the rivalries and split loyalties that must follow.

Fortunately for Gill's son, his barmitzvah reflected the amicable relations between his parents after divorce. 'There was no problem. We were all able to celebrate together,' says Gill.

By way of contrast there was the engagement party and forthcoming wedding of Ronnie's eldest son. Ronnie's former wife has made her position plain according to Gill: 'She hates our guts, both of us. We put on a civilized veneer for the engagement party. As for the wedding, as far as I'm concerned the only people taking part in the ceremony should be the boy and his parents and the girl and her parents, and that's all there is to it.'

Ronnie's son was a young adult by the time his father left his mother, so there was no question of a stepparent taking a major part at his wedding. Arrangements are less clear when a stepparent has a more important role in the life of the family. Common sense should lead to Gill's dictum, but decisions about who gives whom away at a wedding or who has pride of place in any seating arrangements may have to come down to tact, discreet bargainings, a bit of a balancing act.

Delicate handling and some give here and there seem to be the best ways to avoid unwanted slights and collisions. Molly, the divorced Catholic from a large and close-knit family, gave way to her ex-husband's family when she wanted her new partner to attend a funeral. 'It was an uncle of my ex-husband's who had been almost a father to me, and I was very upset. But my ex-husband wanted to go to the funeral and I know the aunt wanted that, much as she likes my new partner. She felt more at ease in that traumatic situation with my ex-husband there.'

What Molly could not contemplate was being at the funeral or at any social occasion, with both men. 'On one occasion, we were asked to a party and the hostess rang and said my ex-husband was also invited. We didn't go. It was too soon after the divorce. There is also the problem that my brother is still a close friend of my ex-husband's, and the Christmas before last my brother had him staying there and brought him over to me. I said, "Don't keep bringing him over" and he said, "You are putting me in an awkward situation." But I found it weird at that time, a tremendous strain. You need to have time to adjust to that sort of thing.'

This seems perfectly reasonable. Friends and relations can

make delicate overtures and act on what they find, at least for a time giving priority to the requirements of the divorced person who is closest to them.

When friends and relations want to exclude a new partner, then other problems arise. Audrey Baker, tutor for the National Marriage Guidance Council, gave this personal account of a family gathering in a talk at a conference on remarriage.

'One of the most uncomfortable occasions for me was my ex mother-in-law's funeral. I went with my two children, as did the lady my ex-husband lives with and her two children. My ex-husband was there of course, and my ex-father-in-law, and all their friends of many years, most of whom had known me as their friends' daughter-in-law. Fortunately I get on well with my ex-husband and his lady, but it was fairly confusing for many of the guests not knowing how to relate to this threesome . . .'

But the ambiguity which made her uncomfortable, and may or may not have confused other guests, was a lesser cause for stress than the next point: 'The person who was not invited and who would not have been welcomed was my husband—and it is in just such situations that the dilemmas which are special to second marriages can surface. My husband is mature and understanding; but in a similar situation with different people, such an event could have become a serious issue.'

Audrey envisages the following reproaches . . . 'You think more of them than you do of me'; 'your place is with me now'; 'you should forget about them.' Like many counsellors, she sees a case for helping remarried couples cope with the complexities of their extended family, and indeed the National Marriage Guidance Council is beginning to offer preparations courses —details of which are given in the next chapter.

EMBARRASSING PROBLEMS

The embarrassment of friends and relations springs partly from the fact that they don't know what the form is. There is the question of taste. Is it bad to refer to an ex-partner in the presence of the new one, even though the subject comes up in conversation? Would it be wrong to invite the ex-partner to a family or social occasion in any circumstance? And how do you behave to them if both ex-partners are present?

The answers to these problems can be disappointingly prosaic. Couples who take the fact of remarriage in their stride can make easy overtures themselves, creating a model for friends and relations to follow. They can be seen in public talking civilly to the ex-partner, sharing some family occasions when appropriate, suggesting to a host that there is no problem, and asking if a new partner might be welcomed at a family funeral.

The uncertainties are greatest when no one is quite sure whether there is a problem or not. Do the ex-couple speak to each other? Has the ex-wife met the new wife? Are friends expected to take sides? To a great extent, the lack of guidelines on social occasions is due to the refusal or inability of couples to take a lead.

The ambiguity of social situations is the element that makes them uncomfortable. But from the point of view of hosts and the outside world there is another, less laudable cause for confusion. It is quite possible to half-fear/half-relish the prospect of witnessing ex-partners meeting on a social occasion. The mixed anticipation is a manifestation of hostility as well as sheer voyeurism. Those who are not divorced may find those who are unsettling, since they create a reminder of the impermanence of marriage, while remarriage or the spectacle of a couple newly in love may inspire less than charitable thoughts and even make the idea of divorce seem rather more enticing.

A cautious host might avoid problems by inviting the ex-partner who has acquired someone new, thus keeping the couple culture intact, or the odd man gets the invitation, since odd men are thin on the ground. This may be no great loss to a woman who has a large circle of supporting friends, but is tough on one who relied on her husband's social life. Harriet comes into the latter category, and having found a new partner thought she had made her position clear to friends. 'I put out a general note on the bush telegraph that my ex-husband and I could be invited to the same party without there being any problem whatsoever. In fact, most people couldn't take the message and they invite one or the other, usually him.'

The voyeurism emerges when an ex-couple does meet face to

face, complete with new partners. The outside world now has the chance for gossip and conjecture or even the prospect of an emotional scene to brighten things up while causing no great harm to the bystanders.

When ex-partners remain friendly, they could be making things simple for other people, but other people are not always so receptive. The hostility experienced by Sue over her closeness with her ex-husband (recorded in the previous chapter) meant that some friends were not seen any more. 'It became a test of their friendship, and in fact most of mine were loyal. But Jim really began again with me, and more or less dropped a lot of people.'

Rejection and criticism do cause pain, but sometimes it is unavoidable. There will always be people who disapprove of the way a marriage ended or of the new life style which one of the partners has acquired.

Anne, who befriended her ex-husband and married a man considerably younger than herself, came in for inevitable gossip. 'There was a fair bit of hostility from relations and friends, but I don't know that I lost any friends in the end. But it's a very great shock to friends of your original marriage if you get a divorce. I think people found it very hard that I was affectionate and friendly to my first husband, and he to me, and there were further difficulties when he became friendly with my second husband as well. That was too much. My first husband's family hadn't been told the full story of our marriage, and they just thought I'd rushed off into the blue, a scarlet woman with a young man. I wrote to my first husband's sister after he died saying how very much I loved him and how deeply upset I was. She told me she'd thought I'd just walked out, suddenly like that. My husband had never told her about us. I think he'd been trying to ignore it, and that was part of the problem of our relationship, that he could never understand, he was too self-involved and he never listened. Now his sister understands more. But there are relatives who virtually won't speak to me still, and make assumptions. It is very difficult to cope with other people who are not privy to your private affairs.'

Rosemary maintains that her unusual household causes no problem, though she recognises that her ex-husband keeps a fairly low profile where their social life is concerned. 'But that's because he's a bit of a loner anyway. Our neighbours and so on all totally accept us. There was never any difficulty with my friends. One of Martin's [Rosemary's second husband] friends can't understand it, and there are people who think all sorts of things about us, but they are not close to us.'

Martin, referring to his one rejecting friend, thinks his reaction was predictable. 'He's a selfish sort of person. He couldn't envisage an amicable break-up. But there are some problems with my parents. They live in the north of England and don't see us much. If they did I think they'd understand a bit more. My father is quite a mild man, but he says I always was the black sheep. All the same, I think they are coming round slowly. They can see that it's all right here.'

The divorce chain, as it is sometimes called, or the remarriage chain, its alternative title, can be seen as a move for the best rather than the worst. It can expand the family network and provide a surprising amount of self-help. That 'haven in the heartless world', the nuclear family, gains a new dimension when it adds on rather than cuts off. The newly extended family might be useful for providing professional help—the new doctor or lawyer in the family, the new builder or decorator. Or it will provide contacts for jobs, giving advice to the children on what or where to study. There might be holiday opportunities, places where members of the family might gather together for its Christmases or special celebrations.

Critics of this kind of self-help society suggest that it produces individuals who are less capable than others of creating sensitive relationships. Research into children of the kibbutz comes to mind—such children are said to be good at avoiding tension and getting on with people at a certain level and that perhaps this makes them lack a certain intensity. These criticisms would have made little sense to the Victorians who idealised large families and did not go greatly for intimate relationships though they did go for stable marriages.

We do want the ability to be intimate and intense, but we also want to retain a sense of family loyalty, to understand what it is to share the caring of the oldest generation, to encourage cooperation in the youngest. It would be no bad thing for children to take on a wide range of loyalties and affection as they grow up, and to understand a little more about other generations in their circle.

Given divorce and remarriage, the chain is surely to be encouraged, and it will flourish best and most easily where parents have buried their differences and made it possible for grandparents and friends to share with them in their funerals and their weddings, their grieving and their celebrations.

Chapter 9
REMARRIAGE AT RISK

Remarrieds are possibly better adjusted for having been through the painful learning process of separation and divorce, according to sociologist Jessie Bernard. She reasons that people are less likely to repeat mistakes if they have learned something about how and why they originally happened. But remarriage soon after divorce among some people—men escaping rejection, for instance, as mentioned in chapter 2—and the high rate of remarriage failure, show that there is no guarantee that people give due time to a learning process, and repeats of old mistakes, or the establishment of new ones, do occur.

In recent years, there has been a steady increase in the failure rate of second or subsequent marriages. Re-divorce as a percentage of all divorces in England, Wales, Scotland and Northern Ireland has risen from 11.6% in 1976 to 20% in 1983.

For women who remarry after a divorce, the likelihood that their new marriage will also end in divorce is twice as high as that for women of the same age marrying for the first time. Men who remarry are one and a half times more likely to divorce again than men of the same age marrying for the first time. The statistics suggest that women are less happy than men in second marriages.

Bernard's work on remarriage was published in the 1950s, when divorce carried more stigma and psychoanalysts tended to pile on the guilt, especially in the direction of women. She quotes one Edmund Berger, author of *Divorce Won't Help* (Harper, 1948), who claimed that the assertive woman was unfeminine, and therefore was afflicted by a 'moral inaptitude' towards marriage. This poor creature was neurotically divorce-prone and so repeated her mistakes in remarriages. If she stayed in an unhappy marriage, she was, presumably, masochistic but she did have moral aptitude.

Today, it would be an easy to turn the spotlight on men instead, and suggest that the 'divorce-prone' amongst them are lacking in the kind of flexibility and sensitivity that modern women want. But we don't have to be macho male or assertive female to repeat life patterns. Dr Jack Dominian of the Marriage Research Centre has said: 'There is no doubt that some people are unsuitable for any marriage—people who are aloof, who find it difficult to accept love or relate to others. So they will find that the problem they faced in the first marriage will continue in a second one.'

People may rush into a second marriage through loneliness, or they have an affair and move in with a new partner without giving themselves time to sort out in their minds some of the things that went wrong in their marriage and the part they contributed. Anyone can settle on a similar partner a second time in the hope of managing differently, or choose someone who might seem to complement personal strengths or weaknesses, sometimes with unrealistic expectations.

Even so, none of these things have to spell disaster. Some people do their homework long before they leave their marriage —like the teacher, Anne, quoted in previous chapters. Others simply take time to grow up and end up happily with someone very similar to a previous partner. Pam, who first married a fellow student, then a man much older than herself and is now happily settled with a man of her own age, considers that all three are rather alike. 'I do think my present husband is much nicer than the previous two, but I would not say he is wildly different from them. It is quite possible that if I had married No. 1 now it would have worked.'

Family therapist Margaret Robinson does not think that marrying the same kind of person again necessarily means making the same mistake. 'If a person hasn't attempted to face his or her own part in the failure of the marriage, or learned from that experience, then they are likely to make the same mistake. If they do learn, they may marry the same kind of person, and this time they are able to manage.'

She finds couples come to her for therapy not knowing whether they want to continue the marriage or not. 'It's a sign of the times. In the past you either went on with it, or got some help in order to go on with it, or you got out.' Some couples come when difficulties in a second marriage begin to look very similar to those that developed in a first marriage, often, Margaret thinks, because there is a failure to achieve intimacy. 'Marriage is a search for intimacy, and when people see they are not finding it second time around they do seek help and they are more realistic about what can be achieved. It seems to me that if the marriage is fulfilling enough the second time, then maybe when difficulties arise they can manage them. People have to learn new patterns, and they can do this more easily with a new partner even if the person is similar.'

When the new partner is not similar, there may still be echoes from the previous relationship. 'We have different relationships with different people, which allow us to express different parts of our personality, and marriage being usually the most intimate relationship we have, there may be aspects of a first marriage present in a second—certain strands of it,' says Margaret.

When things are not going well, the discovery of such strands can be very disturbing. Dora married her second husband, George, after a gap of eighteen years, a big step for a woman in her fifties, a grandmother, who was prepared to move away from her family to a different city to live with her new husband. George, nearing sixty, also a grandparent, was more or less separated from his first wife, and left when he decided he wanted to remarry. To Dora, everything about George seemed totally different from her previous husband. 'I always wanted to look up to a man, because I thought men were superior beings. I wanted literally to look up to them. My first husband was short with blue eyes, and when I left him I thought I could never again go out with a man who was short with blue eyes. So what did I choose a second time? a tall man with straight legs and brown eyes. But I look up to him in more ways than one. My first husband had a minor job. He was a salesman. My second husband is a professional man, and an eminent one.'

The marriage took place four years ago, and almost immediately Dora felt a change in her husband's attitude to her. 'My first husband put me down. He would say humiliating things to me in public. That was one of the reasons I left. Now I find George is very similar. If I'm feeling confident, I let it wash over me, but if I'm feeling down, I'm devastated. I think he is an admirable man, but sometimes I think he is not admirable at all. Many's the time I've thought I've married the same kind of man, even though they are so different in every other way. And I was horrified to think that after all those years of being on my own and having boyfriends who treated me with respect, I had chosen another man who was as rotten as my first husband. You only think of it like that when things are going badly. It makes you stop short. You think you can't possibly have done the same thing again. And then you think, maybe it's you bringing it out in people.'

This is indeed a discomforting thought. Perhaps it's not George who brings similar elements into Dora's second marriage so much as Dora herself, a woman with romantic ideas about male superiority which turn her into a victim. 'I am struggling so hard to find some kind of emotional balance in this marriage that I have chosen, but I haven't come to grips with it. I don't like complaining because I know I lose control and start to scream and then I'm sneered at and told I am illogical. I think his first wife was different from me. She was uncomplaining, she put up with a lot. So perhaps he was different with her. But in one way he was the same. I remember once we were sitting around chatting with his daughter, and suddenly George said, well I think I'll put my feet up, and he left everybody and went off. Now I was with his family, not my daughter. I wouldn't do that if I was with my family and George was the stranger. And his daughter said, don't worry, dad was always like that. He never participated in the household. It made me feel better for the moment, but then I felt angry. It seems to me men rarely leave a wife just to leave a wife. They leave because there is another woman waiting to take them on, and they can go on behaving any way they like.'

While there are women around like Dora, hoping to fulfil romantic fantasies by being attracted to partners who seem aloof and superior, there will be men who feel able to bestow themselves, warts and all, without doing anything about their failings. Both may marry partners who seem different from their previous ones, but they will either behave as they did before, or have similar expectations, with distressing consequences.

Rob is a man who chose someone very different when he married for the second time. While his first wife had wanted more children and he hadn't, his second, divorced, did not want children and was very much a career woman. It is a fairly typical situation today already seen in this book: couple marry young, wife becomes domesticated, husband grows more sophisticated as he rises up the career ladder and wants a more 'liberated' partner to match his new way of life.

'My first wife wanted me to be a family man and go for walks with the children on Sundays, but often it was the day I'd want to unwind alone after a heavy week.'

Rob married his second wife, Ruth, two years after his divorce. Four years later the second marriage also ended in divorce. 'Why did my marriages end? The first is easy to explain. We were growing apart. My view about the second is that it went wrong because I believed in us both having some kind of separate life as well as being together. But I think Ruth wasn't able to handle the freedom. She had this responsible office manager job, and she wanted to please too many people. I was always the one who lost out. For instance, we used to travel to work together, and she would drop me off and pick me up in the evening. Gradually, I was having to wait longer and longer in the evening because somebody wanted something done at work, and she'd get caught up in it. If that had been happening to me, I'd say before a meeting started, I have to leave at a certain time, and I'd go. But she could only say no to me, not to other people. And I could be waiting for an hour and a half.'

This sounds a bit like the reverse of the situation in Rob's first marriage, when he put his own needs before the family. No-body, however, is likely to say of a man that he isn't able to handle freedom, or cannot say no to his boss when he is working to further his career. Rob's first wife is more likely to have said that she felt neglected, overloaded with family duties, and there was no proper sharing.

Just as Rob refused to compromise in his first marriage, there were no compromises in his second. Rob might have travelled home alone, or Ruth could have restricted her late nights to once or twice a week, or at least given some notice of her lateness. Neither seem to have realised that compromise is just as necessary in a liberated marriage as it is in a traditional one.

There was another complication in the form of a mutual friend, a woman, whom Rob sees as 'driving a wedge between me and my wife.' This woman, says Rob, made claims on their social life which he resisted while his wife was torn in his loyalties. The two women would see each other on their own, and again Ruth's time-keeping caused resentment. 'She would stay out late without telling me. It wasn't that I minded, as long as I knew. But she'd promise to be back at nine and turn up not one hour but two hours late.'

Perhaps some of this is jealousy. A career-minded, independent wife may have seemed attractive when Rob was married to a stay-at-home, but the reality was more insecure-making. It sent the marriage downhill.

Says Rob, 'I started to harbour grudges about things. Then she met someone, and I guessed and challenged her to make up her mind what she wanted. If I'd actually put my foot down and said now that's it, you stay with me, I want you here and these are the arrangements from now on, I think she would have stayed. I only say that with hindsight. I didn't do it because a flaw in my character is that when something starts to go wrong, and I am let down, I pull out. I do that in business as well. I did it in my first marriage. But I wanted that one to end. In my second, I didn't. I only wanted her to go because of my character of withdrawing. In reality I was not prepared to fight for what I felt at the time was a lost cause.'

It might still have been a lost cause if Rob had fought. Not only are independent women unlikely to take kindly to being told how to live their social lives, any woman, or man too, will find it difficult to give up somebody in the middle of a love affair. If you really want to save a marriage when there is an affair on the sidelines, you probably have to stick it out, ask for no promises which you know will be broken and will lead to greater deception, and talk through any other conflicts with understanding, or maybe not talk at all for a cooling-down time. Goodwill doesn't always work overnight.

Looking back over his marriage failures, Rob feels he understands the common denominator: 'It is my character. I stop communicating when things are breaking down.' Now, contemplating a third marriage, to a divorced woman with two children, he says, 'My own children said to me "Good" when my second marriage broke up. I didn't know that before. They said she wasn't right for me. They tell me that the woman I am with now is good for me. I think we will end up getting married. She is intellectually far superior to the other two, and more logical.'

Will that be right for Rob? Will an intelligent woman help him make more sense of his desire for an independent partner without feeling insecure about it? Will the presence of her children help?

Rob is certainly prepared to work at it. He likes the new partner's daughter, aged eight, and is happy that she will be living with them. He sees possible conflict with the son, aged twelve, who is at boarding school. On the one hand he talks of 'staying outside and watching until things settle down' as far as the boy is concerned. On the other: 'We are communicating all the time and talking about every single problem, and I will not withdraw this time.'

THE UNCHARTED INSTITUTION

Leaving aside right or wrong choices or flaws in character, remarriage as an institution has many potential built-in stresses. Guilt about causing pain and leaving children, anger towards ex-spouse, worry about making one family income do for two, concern about acquired stepchildren, all put pressure on the new couple.

While therapists and counsellors concentrate on the couple, their unresolved issues from the past and their present personal problems, many researchers are looking at the state of remarriage and its intrinsic challenges. Andrew Cherlin, in his paper 'Remarriage as an Incomplete Institution', includes the following warning: 'Because of the lack of social regulations, each family must devise its own solutions to these problems. The work of establishing rules increases the potential for conflict among family members, and the increased conflict, in turn, increases the likelihood of divorce.'

Whilst acknowledging that remarriage is more complex and indistinctly institutionalised, other sociologists like Fursten-burg and Spanier are less sure that these factors are the main causes of failure, and speculate that researchers overlook the informal and inventive ways in which people compensate for culturally uncharted situations. Their own long-term work with Pennsylvanian couples suggests another hazard. They found a change in expectations after divorce, with a new idea of 'conditional commitment'. This was true of respondents before and after they had remarried.

They suggest that 'people who have divorced not only may be less committed to marital continuity for its own sake, but also that the experience of divorce predisposes individuals to exit from an unhappy (re)marriage . . . Most remarried individuals have demonstrated a willingness or at least a capacity to con-sider divorce as an alternative to continuing an unhappy mar-riage.' Even those who had divorce imposed upon them would be less likely to tolerate a 'low quality' marriage than many never-divorced individuals. Having been through the trauma of divorce once, the cost of doing so again seems smaller, and there is less willingness to put up with partners who cause frustration and unhappiness.

All these recent ideas put greater emphasis on general atti-tudes and the circumstances in which remarried people find themselves. If they are divorce-prone, it is not necessarily because they are neurotic or have chosen the wrong partners. The sheer pressures of remarriage are sufficient in themselves to threaten a relationship, especially when based on conditional commitment.

It is perhaps conditional commitment that makes a couple break up within a few months of getting married, though they have lived together before that for many years—a fairly com-mon occurrence according to Renate Olins of the London Marriage Guidance Council. She suggests that living together is seen as 'fun' by some couples, so that they deny any jarring notes, which emerge once the relationship is given a more legitimate footing. (Of course, increasing numbers of couples prefer to remain unmarried, though they are thoroughly and seriously committed to each other, as are some of the people interviewed for this book. In *Living Together*, authors Clare Dyer and Marcel Berlins define certain types of cohabiting couples as 'married' or 'committed' in their outlook, organising their finances and property just as if they were married.)

Sometimes, the couple are waiting for a divorce and one partner becomes tense, worrying about the other's commitment and perhaps aware of time passing and the reducing possibility of having children. The marriage may finally take place through pressure from this partner, with the optimistic idea that all will be well once it has occurred, though any underlying problems between the couple may remain unresolved.

It is also possible that in these times of ambiguous roles between the sexes, there is a change of attitude about who should or can do what before and after marriage. A husband may no longer expect to share chores or tolerate his wife's social or professional life without him; a wife may no longer approve of her husband spending long hours playing golf or showing little ambition to get on at work, though before the marriage these were not issues that caused friction.

Many second marriages are threatened by issues that caused barely a glimmer of dissent in the early days of the relationship. They can enlarge to major proportions when a couple is into settled domesticity, especially when a child comes along.

Norman and June have been discovering new conflicts since their son was born five months ago. Both are devoted to the new baby, and as discussed earlier, are experiencing problems with Norman's two children from his previous marriage. Now, with June having given up her job, money is tighter and June is looking to Norman for his promised promotion. There is disappointment since it hasn't materialised, and some anger on June's part over Norman's apparent passivity.

Norman is not surprised. 'When we were going to get married, and June was working, one of the things she said she had to do was to be able to respect me. And part of that respect is that I would be able to provide for her in loving care as much as financial looking after. We moved here knowing that promotion wasn't a foregone conclusion, but providing I did the right sort of things, promotion would come. Now my boss has stuck the knife in. I haven't got the promotion and I know June has lost a certain amount of respect for me, because I didn't handle him as she thinks I should have done. She has said to me, could she actually continue to live with somebody for whom she was losing respect?'

This is a sadly stereotyped predicament which can and does occur in any marriage. It would be so much easier if both Norman and June could accept that men do not always have to be assertive, and are often not able to be, and may even command respect when they are not. But remarriage adds further complications. There is the sign of conditional commitment when June wonders whether she can live with somebody who does not meet her standards, and there is leftover business from the time of the divorce. Says Norman, 'She doesn't feel that I am strong or assertive enough with my boss or with my former wife. And that was all part of it. In between the time that the divorce came through, and before our marriage, she saw me at the lowest I have ever been because of the problems with my former wife. And I think there is a certain loss of respect towards me because I couldn't handle the situation. I'd felt so suicidal and guilty. I didn't know what to do, and there was a certain amount of respect lost there.'

Perhaps June felt that her husband's conflict reflected a lack of conviction about the move to the new relationship? Perhaps the anger she feels towards him is basically due to this? Underneath the need for a strong man may be a fear of uncertainty and a need to guarantee that everything is under control.

And there is a further complication through remarriage. The new job and new life meant moving to another area, many miles away from a troublesome ex-wife. In this case it is a village, not very remote, but not comfortable for a woman who has just given up a full-time job which involved travelling round the country. Says June, 'I wanted the baby so much, and because of Norman's reversed vasectomy I never really believed we could have a child of our own. Now I'm absolutely terrified of leaving the baby. I'm completely isolated, there's no family nearby. We live with open country behind us, and there have been a couple of rapes round here. When Norman is away I'm on a knife edge.'

Fortunately, both recognise that they need help, and they are receiving counselling and also attend sessions at a local branch of the Stepfamily Association. Says Norman, 'When this happens to a lot of people in their first marriage, they break up. They know something's wrong but they won't seek outside help because that's an admission of failure. Whereas having failed already in people's eyes by having a marriage go wrong, I've no qualms as far as that goes. If we can't handle something because we're so intense, we've got to turn to other people.'

Not everyone would see a second failure in this light. There may be a vested interest in showing other people that all is going well in a new marriage. But perhaps there is also an alarm system that operates earlier a second time. The warning signs are seen and heeded. When there is an underlying attitude of conditional commitment, there may be little time to waste before one party or the other decides to pull out.

MONEY AND CHILDREN

Research has shown that finance plays a greater part in the failure of remarriage than infidelity—a common reason for the break-up of first marriages. In families where there is money to fight over, it is likely to cause more disputes than do the children. A woman who remarries may be better off than one who does not, but a man who remarries may have to support two homes. Second wives become extremely bitter over this, as do husbands when it was the wife who left the marriage, possibly to live with someone else. Conduct can be taken into account over maintenance payments, but the courts rarely follow this up because of the consequent suffering of the children.

Pam, when married to her second husband, recalls the financial strains: 'Two of his children were at private schools, and his ex-wife said she would sting him for every penny. And she did. She was always telephoning and complaining to me. I could see she had the right to be bitter because I had stolen her husband, but that didn't stop me from being resentful. Though I was earning, we were very short of money, and it seemed deeply unfair that we couldn't get on with our own married life and set up a decent home without this terrible burden. It undoubtedly contributed to the failure of our own marriage.'

Women marrying for the second time may also have different ideas about their financial autonomy, having learned to manage their own financial affairs after a divorce. They may be more wary than first wives about sharing all resources, especially if they are earning themselves or have assets from a previous marriage.

Husbands sensitive to recently-discovered materialistic elements in ex-wives may be hurt or resentful if they feel their new partner shows less than perfect trust in them. But they too may hold back on information about their assets, having been bitten the first time, and researchers have found a reluctance in men to revise wills, insurance and property assets. The optimism with which people enter into a new relationship offers little preparation for such issues, though the built-in dangers would seem obvious.

Inevitably, the problems caused by children in a remarriage can sometimes be insurmountable. Len, whose second marriage was ending after eight years, blames the failure on his second wife's youngest son of fifteen, though there were clearly partnership difficulties too. 'She has always been too soft on him. I wouldn't have stood for such things with my own children. He was a difficult child, wanting a lot of her attention. He always wanted a light on all night in his bedroom, and there was no need for it. Now the last straw is that he has become violent, smashing things in the house, breaking windows and the front door in. I said he would have to go and live with his father as I wouldn't have him in my home any longer. He went for a while but he kept coming back so I changed the locks.'

This sorry state of affairs suggests inflexibility and insensitivity towards a troubled child. Even if Len had tried to be generous at times, he lacked understanding in a difficult situation, till it got to the point where he quite reasonably took measures to protect his property. Though he says there was 'nothing wrong' with his relationship with his wife, clearly a lot of things were wrong where the boy was concerned, and Len's wife will have needed support that does not seem to have been forthcoming.

Perhaps in this case the child became the scapegoat, an easy target for Len's and his wife's dissatisfaction with the marriage, so that no confrontation about their own relationship was necessary. Sometimes, a mother with custody of her children can present a 'closed system' to a new husband, making it difficult for him to penetrate the tight-knit family bond that has developed since separation and divorce. A new man coming in can feel as excluded, and as jealous, as any child.

Problems such as Len's and others revealed here are beginning to be recognised by counsellors and therapists as common hazards of the state of remarriage which exacerbate any personal difficulties a couple might have. Courses are being set up for people entering remarriage to help them deal with their situations in positive ways. Details about these are given in the following final chapter.

Chapter 10
HELP!

This final chapter looks at the many ways, both public and private, in which people can be helped and can help themselves and their loved ones through divorce and remarriage and the business of being stepparents.

Public help comes in several forms, including counselling, psychotherapy, conciliation and special courses. Undoubtedly the biggest potential help with divorce will be through the creation of family courts and a nationwide conciliation service, explained as follows.

DIVORCE AND AFTER

FAMILY COURTS

Traditionally, the legal profession has acted in an adversarial role in divorce, as in other matters when people are in conflict. To a lawyer, defending a client in a criminal case might not seem so different from defending a client in a divorce case, but after the procedure is over divorced people may still find they have to cope with each other's existence, and children cannot be cut into legal pieces and served up to support principles of crime and punishment.

This is just one of many reasons for the setting up of family courts which would take divorce out of the courts that deal in criminal matters and into a specialised structure with trained judges and lay magistrates. Family courts were recommended by the Finer report on one-parent families in 1974 and there are signs that at last, in the 1980s, they may come into being.

The form that family courts will take is still at the debating stage. Martin Richards in his book written with Jacqueline Burgoyne, *Divorce Matters*, looks to New Zealand as the place with the system most appropriate to British needs. There, first contact with the court is informal, with selected judges who have knowledge and experience of both social and psychological aspects of family life. Children are represented by specially trained barristers.

To start with, if there is any dispute, a couple are referred to a counselling coordinator offering information and counselling. She (at present all are women) will explore and define areas of disagreement with both partners separately. If all goes well the couple make a joint application for divorce.

If things are not resolved, the couple each see their lawyers for a formal application to the court and then the counselling coordinator refers the couple to a conciliator. The next step, if this fails to produce agreement, is for a counsel to be appointed to represent any child of the marriage. A child psychiatrist or psychologist might also be brought in. From this will arise a mediation conference with parents, solicitors, child's counsel, the counselling coordinator and the judge. Such adversarial devices as cross examination or the giving of evidence are avoided. Finally there is an appeal procedure if the legal decision is strongly resisted by either one or both of the divorcing adults.

This may not be the system that will ultimately be used in the United Kingdom, but something like it, incorporating expert child representation, some degree of informality in the courts and conciliation services will finally emerge. The advent of family courts will help to reduce some of the anguish and bitterness of divorce that in so many cases continue long after the divorce is made absolute.

CONCILIATION SERVICES

A conciliation service attached to family courts was part of the recommendation of the Finer report on one-parent families in 1974. In the event, the conciliation service came first, developing piecemeal in different parts of the country, though it is still not nationwide. Some conciliation services are run by probation officers and are attached to county courts. In some of these courts they are a compulsory part of the divorce procedure.

Others are run independently, often by voluntary organisations, and are coordinated under the National Family Conciliation Service.

Conciliation is neither counselling nor reconciliation. Finer described it as 'assisting the parties to deal with the consequences of the established breakdown of their marriage whether resulting in divorce or separation, by reaching agreement or . . . reducing the area of conflict upon custody, support, access to and education of children, financial provision, the disposition of the matrimonial home, lawyers' fees and every other matter arising from the breakdown which calls for a decision on future arrangements.' That just about wraps up every trouble-making item on the post-divorce agenda, plus savings of millions of pounds in legal disputes and the psychological and social gains which are beyond price.

Conciliation is no easy option. Indeed, conciliators report that parents in disagreement sometimes propose that they let the court decide, rather as if the decision-making is too much for them even though they risk getting landed with conditions they find unworkable. The aim of conciliation is to gear people into thinking through their situation and making their own decisions.

One area in which conciliation can be very effective is that of custody. Sole custody to one parent is very much the norm, despite concern that this easily leads to the other parent losing contact with the child. A Law Commission study in 1986 urged judges to increase joint custody orders from the present 5% or under, and to see them as a creative answer not a compromise solution. A proper conciliation service can ensure that parents look clearly at the consequences for children of any custody decision they make and the children themselves can be consulted and their views represented.

Conciliators often work in pairs, in order that one can maintain neutrality while the other can offer support when appropriate. There may be individual interviews first, but ultimately the work is done at joint interviews, or sometimes with the whole family. The main aim is negotiation. In one kind of scheme, divorcing couples and their solicitors attend a 'mediation appointment' at the court with a probation officer or social worker. An innovation in Britain is the use of one solicitor to mediate between the couple, which cuts down the adversarial role.

The presence of a solicitor at conciliation sessions makes a great deal of sense. But there are critics of conciliation in general and of the presence of solicitors in particular. Some fear the consultation will become too 'legal' in its approach. Women, particularly, may feel at a disadvantage when there is a strong emphasis on legalities and hard bargaining, and there are suspicions that conciliation works in favour of men, especially if the conciliator reinforces the idea that women are more malleable. Another weakness is that one spouse might take advantage of the other's stress, and a little emotional blackmailing is not beyond the bounds of possibility. It is also possible that greater use of joint custody orders reduces a woman's bargaining power while in no way diminishing the traditional male ability to dictate financial terms. In America, some courts employ psychiatrists or mental health experts to alleviate these problems.

Overall, no one would doubt the usefulness of the service. Miracles it does not perform, but as Thelma Fisher, who chairs the National Family Conciliation Council, says: 'the best discussions lead to a truly integrative solution which is more than a compromise; [though] more often a *quid pro quo* is the best that can be achieved. It is however quite surprising to witness the moment when a battle, which seems unresolvable, suddenly resolves over some gesture of compromise which seems trivial to an outsider but which represents an important balance of prestige to each partner.'

Conciliation is a means to working through the no-go areas, which can be anything from who gets the family photographs to how is Christmas to be carved up for the children. While a couple can get stuck, a good conciliator can suggest some ways forward long before the case comes to the court and the official judgement.

COUNSELLING AND PSYCHOTHERAPY

The first port of call for people distressed over marital problems is often the GP, who may or may not be trained in coping with such matters. At best, he or she will realise that time and attention are what the patient wants; at worst the offering will be that old standby, the tranquilliser.

The most appropriate treatment in many cases is counselling or psychotherapy, both of which have fewer side effects and longer benefits than drugs. Counselling differs from conciliation in that the latter is primarily to do with coming to some kind of agreement over divorce and child custody, while the former in terms of marital conflict is concerned with coming to some kind of personal understanding of the problems in a relationship. Talking to another person helps to get things into perspective and removes some of the heat and hate that may arise over marital breakdown. It is also a useful preparation for the future, with or without a new partner. The prospect of loneliness is better dealt with through counselling than through a desperate and ill-judged bid to form a new relationship too quickly.

Counselling works best with people who are prepared to reflect honestly about their difficulties and are willing to explore, experiment and change. Dramatic improvements rarely occur, but perceptions may shift and feelings may alter accordingly. The rewards are a greater ability to be flexible and to solve personal problems, an increase in self-understanding and self-esteem, and improved relationships with others.

Many voluntary organisations offer counselling, including religious-based ones, which are more likely to work towards reconciliation than divorce. National Marriage Guidance counsellors increasingly see individuals wanting to divorce, as well as couples seeking a way to end their relationship and remarried couples trying to cope with the complications of old and current family commitments. Probation officers, social workers and conciliation services might offer counselling after divorce too.

Where counselling is needed, but rarely offered, is in the workplace. Counselling at work would be a way of offering help to men, who tend to be more deprived of social support following divorce than women and who are more diffident about seeking help through the various existing agencies. Counselling might even reduce absenteeism in women as well as men if it can replace such painkillers as alcohol and tranquillisers.

And workplace nurseries as part of a programme of better childcare facilities would be another way of reducing the stress of divorce and single parenthood.

Where counselling tends to take place over a number of weeks or months and is often available at moderate cost or free, psychotherapy consumes more time, and also a lot more money, being hard to come by on the National Health Service. Psychotherapy aims to go deeper than counselling. Problems are examined in greater depth, which may be necessary where the pain and anger are threatening to overwhelm. Some people find they can only come to terms with their anger, fear, sense of insecurity, guilt or self-pity by giving themselves time with a sympathetic listener who will intervene to point out irrational thinking and over-emotional responses and help point the way to a calmer and more positive future. Counselling will do this, but psychotherapy offers the opportunity to explore old mistakes and change patterns of behaviour usually by going into greater detail about past influences and providing the opportunity to relive some of the experiences.

Marital therapy, where couples are seen together, tends to be more common when there is some hope of reconciliation. Family therapy, involving various members of both generations, again tends to work for reconciliation, though it is also helpful in remarriage (see below).

DEMARRIAGE CEREMONIES

There is a fairly new kind of therapeutic experience offered to couples on divorce, and that is the divorce or demarriage ceremony. Birmingham probation service is one of several trying this end-of-marriage experiment. A divorce court welfare officer sees both parties together and helps them to talk about both the good and the bad times they've had and the things they have to forgive in one another. The couple are then told to say goodbye and are left alone for a short while. The officer returns and invites each partner to make a formal, solemn statement to the effect that they recognise that their marriage is ended, that they are saying goodbye and letting each other go.

Such ceremonies are about accepting loss and failure with simplicity and dignity. There are critics who suggest that they are more the province of the Church than of probation officers who do not necessarily have a spiritual relationship with their clients. In fact, there is room for such ceremonies in many walks of life—psychotherapists, counsellors, conciliators are all in a position to offer some kind of balm to ease the pain and mark the occasion. Perhaps the best place for a demarriage ceremony would be in the family courts.

DIVORCE EXPERIENCE COURSES

These are short-term programmes that offer individuals a chance to share opinions and experiences with a group of perhaps two dozen other people about to separate or be divorced. David Straker, a probation officer in Leicester, was one of the first people to inaugurate divorce experience courses spread over three separate evening sessions. The first evening concentrates on the adult's emotional experience of divorce, and participation is in the form of group discussions. The second focuses on legal aspects and on the third evening parents are invited to bring children who can take part in discussions with a welfare officer in a separate room. Parents on this last evening listen to a presentation on children's needs.

There are similar courses in other areas. In Nottingham, the probation service and marriage guidance council have run a four-evening programme on 'splitting up' with about ten people taking part. Participants have the option of forming a self-help group to continue meeting afterwards.

THE CHILDREN

EDUCATION ON DIVORCE

One child in every five born today will have to cope with parental divorce before the age of sixteen if present trends continue. Some of these children will probably have a voice in decisions about their future through the family courts. It would help them considerably if the subject were given an airing away from the hothouse atmosphere of home, and the obvious place would be at school.

In America, courses and counselling programmes are increasing in popularity in schools. Linda Bird Francke, in her book *Growing Up Divorced*, describes such projects as a course entitled 'Who Gets me for Christmas?' offered to pupils at a New York middle school, and a pantomime featuring a furry character called Orby who enlists help from elementary school pupils in Indiana on how to solve his problems with divorce. Some teachers counsel students from broken homes individually, others provide workshops in schools after hours. In Marin County, California, the Center for the Family in Transition conducts six-week workshops for teachers on setting up counselling groups and on how to bring divorce-related subjects into the curriculum.

In Britain things are nowhere near as advanced. Some polytechnics offer subject courses to trainee teachers on personal and social education. Some schools offer pupils courses on preparation for marriage, childcare and other aspects of family life, perhaps with something on divorce thrown in. The emphasis is on training for adulthood rather than on dealing with the stresses of current family life. But even then the 'life skills' subjects have little status and are mainly directed at the non-academic children.

There is room for both kinds of education in the classroom—the development of ideas about personal choice (why we choose our partners, what we expect of them, how we can destroy relationships through indifference or unreasonable demands) and the acknowledgment of the painful experience of parents divorcing. From the latter, using the children's own feelings and observations, can come some real learning about the former.

Schools can also help in other ways. Teachers can ease the embarrassment of names when a parent remarries by being open and relaxed about the subject. Schools can offer to send reports and notices to two addresses when parents part. But the first step is to alert the teachers so that they can present the divorced and remarried family as a fact of life, however regrettable that may be.

REMARRIAGE

PREPARATION COURSES

Like divorce experience courses, these tend to be run as workshops, providing information and some counselling. An experimental remarriage counselling course conducted by Moira Fryer, tutor consultant to the National Marriage Guidance Council, involved six couples, all with stepchildren. All defined their major problem as being in the area of stepparenting, mostly focusing on the behaviour of one child.

There were three sessions at weekly intervals, at the end of which came a realisation that there might be greater complications at work than simply problems with stepchildren, who could easily be made to take the blame when there were stresses in the marriage itself.

Courses run by educationalist and marriage guidance counsellor Rachel Gilliatt and educational psychologist Gerv Leyden have been held in Nottingham over seven weekly sessions, with about six couples. Members work in twos, changing pairings often, and then report back to the whole group. There are sessions exploring the roles and expectations of stepmothers and stepfathers, stepchildren and the family group. Use is made of role play, with participants taking part as characters in various remarriage situations. Games and imaginative exercises help to create insight into the feelings of children. From these experiences, participants have a better perception of their situations and are able to evolve certain new and beneficial rules of behaviour.

Group meetings along these lines first developed in America, and a consistent finding was that couples were poorly prepared for the problems they had to face. The most commonly discussed concerns in groups run by Lillian Messinger and her team in Toronto, were transition from marriage to separation; a redefinition of identity from being divorced to being remarried; ties between first and second marriages; roles of adults, children and stepchildren; and previous marital status.

Marriage guidance councils and probation services are the

organisations most likely to hold courses in Britain, but there are also private counselling institutions offering one-day or weekend seminars run by social workers or psychotherapists.

Though courses tend to be called 'preparation for remarriage', in practice they attract people who are already remarried and experiencing some difficulties. It is not so easy to catch those planning to remarry. However, the Church recognises a role in the education of couples for marriage, and in some dioceses remarriage is included in that education. Michael Hare Duke, Bishop of St Andrews, stresses the importance of the Church learning from the work of marriage counselling and sees a part that it could play in sustaining good relations between ex-partners and in improving the quality of the newly extended family.

FAMILY THERAPY

Remarriages, and first marriages too of course, may focus problems on a particular member of the family and sometimes the others will fail to see that they have created a scapegoat when everyone concerned needs a change of attitude in order to restore peace and harmony. Family therapy may at different times include the adult couple, children and stepchildren, and perhaps even an ex-partner in order to bring out different points of view on the way people are interacting. There are some therapists who are prepared to bring in grandparents and other members of the family too.

Family therapists may concentrate on the phase in the family life cycle being experienced by their clients—for instance, the common problems arising when a father of late adolescent children marries a woman who has never before been married. There is scope for a broad look at family life and so less concentration on any individual.

The main disadvantage with family therapy is that it is usually available only through private psychotherapists and it is costly in time and money. The techniques are well suited to the complexities of stepfamily relationships, though work in this area is fairly new and still developing.

THE NATIONAL STEPFAMILY ASSOCIATION

This self-help organisation deserves a section to itself because it is unique in serving the needs of people in stepfamilies. It was set up in 1983 and advises stepparents and stepchildren. It has a nationwide telephone counselling service and branches in various parts of the country where informal weekly meetings take place. Here talk will be about custody, maintenance, child discipline, anything that comes up from the experiences and interests of the members present. Since this is a self-help group and advice comes from the couples and individuals gathered together, it may be inconsistent, and by no means always wise. But the sharing of problems is therapeutic and group leaders are usually people with special experience who can offer their extra knowledge. There are plans to run training courses and to offer special courses for social workers.

SELF HELP

This section offers a run-through of personal ways to handle situations in divorce and in remarriage. It is not so much a matter of do's and don'ts, as possible approaches to take and certain guidelines to bear in mind.

DIVORCE

Use a conciliation service. Agreement on issues saves time, stress and money. If an agreement is made by the parties concerned it is more likely to be observed than one imposed by a solicitor or court decision. Find a solicitor who is experienced in family law. It is in your interests to see that your partner gets a suitable solicitor too. If financial means are limited it is worth applying for legal aid.

Divorce experience courses offer practical advice and a chance to share views with others in similar situations.

If you have difficulty in adjusting to being divorced or feel driven by sustained anger as well as grief, a marriage guidance counsellor or psychotherapist can help. Asking for help is not a sign of weakness, it is a sign of strength. It may also make all the difference between going into a second relationship successfully or adding to the remarriage divorce rates.

Grieving, however, is a natural part of any distressing experience, and is not a sickness unless it continues unabated for a long period of time and produces permanent apathy. Moods of regret and loss usually come and go, decreasing gradually over several months or even a couple of years.

It is helpful to figure out what attracted you to your ex-partner, what held you together and what each of you contributed to the break-up. This means a move away from thinking in terms of the guilty party, of apportioning blame, of thinking you were doing it right while the other one was doing it wrong. It also makes explanations to the children easier and more authentic.

CHILDREN AND SEPARATION

Uncertainty is worse than knowing the worst. Even very young children need to be told what's going on, including the fact that separation is sad even if it might in the end turn out for the best. Unhappiness is better shared, and to hide distress from children makes it impossible for them to express their own unhappiness. But there is a limit. It would be unfair to put pressure on the children to be the comforters. Sharing is the key word.

That goes for financial difficulties too. Children should know when such difficulties exist, and if they offer to make sacrifices it is better that everyone does rather than that a parent should make sacrifices alone.

Children should not only know about the separation, they should also be asked about who they want to live with. But it does depend on the age and maturity of the children, and again too much pressure is as unfair as too much freedom of choice.

Children nearly always hope that parents will get together again. Parents have to face this one as best they can. Storybooks telling about divorce help demonstrate that there are others in the same boat.

Antisocial behaviour is common in children of divorce. They

need to be treated tenderly when they are angry or withdrawn. On the other hand, it is important to express disapproval when they are provocative and aggressive. This can be done in reasoned tones, no threats but some communication about the fact that hurting people is uncalled for.

ACCESS AND CUSTODY

It is tempting to use children as go-betweens when relations with an ex-partner are strained. This not only creates torn loyalties and greater unhappiness, it allows children an ability to exploit the situation both ways.

Joint custody is a way of expressing publicly that though two adults no longer wish to live with each other, they continue to be parents. As emotions cool down, both parents can talk to children about the good things that were shared in the past, family holidays, outings, etc. It doesn't help to rewrite their history.

Children will readily support a good relationship between their parents after divorce. This is much easier to accept than a bad one, when they might feel torn in their loyalties or even suspect that they are to blame for the break-up.

It may be irresistible, but punishing the other parent by depriving him or her of access to the children should be resisted. It punishes them too.

A newly separated parent might find that visits upset the children and be tempted to curtail them. What is really upsetting the children is the separation of the parents, which is a perfectly reasonable reaction. While a short-term curtailment of visits is acceptable if emotions run high, there will be greater long-term upset if children are deprived of visits generally or feel they are pawns in the power struggle between their parents.

An ex-partner visiting may seem like an intrusion, especially when there is a new relationship in the offing. But the children are not divorced, and they need the visits even if their parent doesn't.

Sometimes children declare a refusal to visit their non-custodial parent. This may be an expression of anger towards both parents and should not be taken as their permanent point of view. If children profess to hate a parent it is usually within the context of frustrated love no matter what the other parent may want to think.

Problems of access are most acute at the beginning. Once a routine is established they begin to resolve. A reasonably regular schedule of visiting helps, as does a timetable that is respected.

Special treats have their place, but relationships work best during ordinary living time. Money might be better spent on making adequate room for an overnight stay rather than on luxuries.

EX-PARTNERS

The most important thing is to keep him or her informed of changes in visiting time and also any other event that will in some way affect relations, such as remarriage, moving house, holiday plans.

When an ex-partner calls round to collect a child, an offer of a cup of tea signals at least a willingness to call a truce. Some people take longer to grieve and get over negative feelings than others. It would be unfair to try to force friendship too soon—for instance, a partner who leaves for someone new might want to retain contact with an ex-partner before the ex-partner has really come to terms with the situation.

Offers of goodwill and peace-makings may not get a positive response at first. It can take a while to penetrate resentment and suspicion. Endurance may be needed.

Rivalry and competitiveness towards an ex-partner only prolong the agony of ill-feeling.

PARENTS, CHILDREN AND STEPPARENTS

Arrangements involving the children are best discussed without the children present, so that parents and stepparents work in agreement and children are not caught in the crossfire. Of course older children can be consulted too.

Problems of discipline between two households can also be discussed between the parents, plus decisions about pocket money, etc. If there is an agreement about rules between the adults, it is easier for children to stick to them. If there is an agreement to differ, then both parents should respect that conclusion and tell children to do so too.

Children may want love and acceptance from stepparents, but they also want the same from both their parents. This may seem greedy, but it is no more unreasonable than parents who want their children to accept the new stepparent unconditionally and sometimes want them to switch loyalties to the stepparent. Stepparents are additions, not replacements.

If children want to talk about their absent parent, the best thing the listening parent can do about personal hurt and anger is to admit it. But as a statement of fact not an accusation. Demonstrate that you respect the fact he or she is still a parent with parental rights, including the right to be loved by offspring.

If the absent parent obstinately remains absent despite overtures and invitations, try to express regret or disapproval in neutral tones. Yes, you do think it wrong but yes, the invitation remains open.

Discourage any child who tries to be the peace-maker between his parents. The temptation to persuade the child to take your side will be too great.

Recognise that teenagers may not want to visit because they genuinely have other things to do. Teenagers in most families spend less time with their parents than they did when they were younger.

Don't get trapped into taking sides if the children criticise a stepparent. It is reasonable to say that he or she is not your favourite person, but that person still needs to be respected as someone who is important to the other parent and who is also trying hard to be a good stepparent.

If the children express criticisms or show distress after a visit to the other parent and stepparent, sort it out first with the adults and then bring the children into the discussion. Don't use the children as messengers.

If a child lets drop the information that he or she has been talking to an adult friend of yours or a relative about the family, don't see it as disloyalty. An outside listener can add some fresh air to tired old arguments.

Stepmothers don't become mothers overnight, especially if they have never had children of their own. The same goes for stepfathers.

Don't expect stepchildren to offer instant love. Dr Spock of infant care fame and a stepfather himself suggests that step-parents tell a child that they know they are unwanted—'that way, children don't have to feel guilty about their feelings.'

Children need to be asked about their feelings about having different names if they don't volunteer information themselves. They might not be bothered, but it would be better to know.

Stepparents need to go easy on the discipline, especially in the early days. Better to let the biological parents handle it. They will be forgiven more quickly.

If there are two sets of children from different marriages in the house, there may be a need for different rules for each set of children. For instance, those used to having a light on at night should be allowed it, just as a visiting child would be allowed this simple comfort.

If stepchildren don't live up to the unspoken house rules, cultivate a low-key response. Make a list if several items of behaviour irritate, and decide which are worth making into an issue. (This is also a moment to examine personal standards to see whether the fuss is or isn't justified.) Unacceptable table manners might be dealt with like this: 'Now you lot, no more smash and grab today. I'll do the serving and next time you can repay the compliment.' This sets the tone for future reminders. Broken biscuits or half-eaten yogurts left under the bed might be corrected with the offering of a large tray or bin and an explanation about mice not being your favourite animals. You could of course stop buying biscuits or yoghurt or say food in bedrooms is out of bounds. There are alternatives to threats and reprimands.

CO-EXISTING WITH GRANDPARENTS

Ex-in-laws remain grandparents just as ex-partners remain parents. Keep them informed of family movements and prepare them for change—moving house, changing schools, for instance. Grandparents welcome the sense of feeling included.

Sometimes grandparents appear to be meddling. Try to offer humorous tolerance rather than reproofs.

Don't expect grandparents to become instant stepgrandparents. Some need time to adjust.

Provide a few hints about being even-handed when it comes to presents and cards for the grandchildren and stepgrandchildren. 'He/she is always delighted when you send a birthday card' is a way of making suggestions.

Some grandparents try to use money as power. They'll do so less if they feel they are able to participate more as grandparents and as stepgrandparents.

TELLING FRIENDS

Ambiguity breeds uncertainty. Make the current position clear by sending a card announcing a change of address and new partner where appropriate.

If you have no objection to meeting an ex-partner socially, include a message on the card to that effect, with the address of the ex-partner—i.e. 'We're still friends and there's no problem about meeting socially.'

In company when conversation turns to children, divorce or other topics where there might be misreadings or confusion, simply explain your personal position to those present if you contribute your own comments to the conversation.

If you want to convey that it's all right for others to refer to an ex-partner in your presence, refer to him or her yourself.

SELF-PROTECTION—PREMARITAL PACTS

This final note on self-help is one that is unfamiliar in British society but well-known in America. There, lawyers are being asked to draw up premarital pacts for couples before they marry in the hope that should the marriage fail the divorce will be clean and reasonably uncostly.

This business-like approach to romance is more common in second marriages because there may be more money at stake, more property and business interests. Some professional men have practices they wish to protect, children from previous marriages to whom they wish to leave an inheritance. They may also have vivid memories of a past divorce which cost them dearly.

Professional women may also have assets to protect, especially if some of them marry men younger than themselves who are less self-sufficient economically. Two lawyers are needed to represent both parties and their individual interests. There is no guarantee that partners will stick to the agreement if the crunch finally comes and it would be very difficult for a court to enforce it. But the exercise encourages some honest thinking.

Even if premarital pacts never catch on in Britain, there is a place for non-marriage contracts to provide some protection to couples who cohabit. The way things are, if one partner buys the house in his (more likely to be his) own name and pays the mortgage, then the other partner has to prove that the intention was for her to have a share. While she's trying to prove it, there is nothing to stop the owning partner from selling up over her head. So a contract from the start that any property will be in both names, that insurance policies, shares etc. are in joint names, that separate savings are acknowledged as separate, can save an awful lot of trouble.

Such ideas may sound distasteful and speak of distrust between couples, but perhaps they presage a totally new approach to marriage, one that is based on the importance of stability, continuity, mutual respect and even a tiny bit of distancing. Maybe if such things become more valued than passion and self-fulfilment, there will be fewer remarriages, and the ones that do take place will be the ones that last.

ADDRESSES

National Association Of Citizens' Advice Bureaux
Myddleton House,
115–123 Pentonville Road,
London N1
Tel: 01 883 2181

Scottish Association of Citizens' Advice Bureaux
82 Nicholson Street
Edinburgh 8
Tel: 031 667 0156

Northern Ireland Association of Citizens' Advice Bureaux
2 Annadale Avenue
Belfast 7
Tel: Belfast 640011

Solicitors Family Law Association
154 Fleet Street
London EC4A 2HX
Tel: 01 353 3290

National Family Conciliation Council
155 High Street
Dorking
Surrey RH4 1AD
Tel: 0306 882754

National Marriage Guidance Council
Little Church Street
Rugby CV21 3AP
Tel: 0788 73241

London Marriage Guidance Council
76A New Cavendish Street
London WIM 7LB
Tel: 01 580 1087

Scottish Marriage Guidance Council
26 Frederick Street
Edinburgh EH2 2JR
Tel: 031 225 5006

Northern Ireland Marriage Guidance Council
76 Dublin Road
Belfast BT2 7HP
Tel: 0232 223454

Catholic Marriage Advisory Council
15 Lansdowne Road
London W11
Tel: 01 794 5222

Catholic Marriage Advisory Council
18 Park Circus
Glasgow 3
Tel: 041 332 4914

Catholic Marriage Advisory Council
4 Corry Square
Newry
Co. Down
Tel: 0693 3577

London Jewish Marriage Council
23 Ravenshurst Avenue
London NW4
Tel: 01 203 6311

National Coordinating Committee for Parents under Stress
29 Newmarket Way
Hornchurch
Essex
Tel: 0602 819423

National Council for Saturday Parents
Elfrida Hall
Campshill Road
Lewisham
London SE13 6QU
Tel: 01 852 7123 (mornings only)

National Council for One Parent Families
255 Kentish Town Road,
London NW5
Tel: 01 267 1361

Gingerbread
35 Wellington Street
London WC2
Tel: 01 240 0953

National Stepfamily Association
162 Tenison Road
Cambridge CB1 2DP
Tel: 0223 460312 (helpline: 0223 460313)

Families Need Fathers
B. M. Families
London WC1N 3XX
Tel: 01 852 7123

MIND (National Association of Mental Health)
22 Harley Street
London W1N 2ED
Tel: 01 637 0741

British Association of Psychotherapy
121 Hendon Lane
London N3 3PR
Tel: 01 346 1747

Institute of Family Therapy
43 New Cavendish Street
London w1
Tel: 01 935 1651

British Association of Counselling
37a Sheep Street
Rugby
Warwickshire
Tel: 0788 78328

IN CONCLUSION . . .

when I began writing this book, AIDS was something that happened to homosexual men in Haiti and San Francisco. The Africa explosion was more rumour than fact. The risk to heterosexuals was barely considered.

Today, we are more knowledgeable and more fearful because of it. A generation that grew up in the midst of sexual permissiveness is now trying to come to terms with sexual caution. We are not quite at the stage when we actually value virginity, but celibacy is no longer suspect. Marriage, fidelity, stability are words coming back into fashion. Young people, as someone put it, are no longer in the 'me' generation, but are trying to become the 'we' generation, making marriages work by working harder at them.

Does this mean that divorce and remarriage will go out of fashion? Possibly, though they surely won't go out of existence. There will, of course, always be unbearable marriages, people genuinely making impossible choices. We rightly fear the rigidity of puritanism. High-minded judgements should not condemn people to damaging relationships for life, any more than they should turn a healthy need for sexual exploration into forbidden temptation. But the search for passion and total fulfilment may be replaced, or at least be lower in the priorities than acquiring tolerance, generosity, forbearance and understanding, the boring, plodding things that make a failing marriage pull itself together again and most ordinary marriages remain in one piece.

There is a terrible, hidden irony here. All the divorces and remarriages recorded in this book have had to employ those very same qualities in order to balance the past with the present, the old with the new. Many of the couples whose stories are recorded have had to suffer the awesome stages of stepfamily development suggested in chapter four, and to witness the upheavals and possible distress of their children and their partners' children. They have had to work hard for their marriage.

Some will have failed to do so, and have suffered or are still suffering because of it. Spotting the mistakes is easy enough when you are reading the words or listening to them for that matter. Sometimes, as I listened to the people I interviewed for this book, I thought of all the effort and emotional energy demanded of remarriage. Could it, perhaps, have gone into making the first marriage work?

Such an idea is more acceptable for a 'we' society than one that regards it as a moral duty to end a marriage for an intense love affair or the urge to find self-esteem. Perhaps the Seven Year Itch (and it doesn't have to be in the seventh year) could be regarded instead as the Seven Year Rebellion. A similar pattern exists in earlier stages of human development. Infants begin with dependence on a single other person, and seek separation with a mixture of fear and resentment. Adolescents detach themselves from the values of their parents, sometimes with condemnation and disillusionment. Maybe young marrieds go through a similar process—of dependence, of disappointment and anger, which is a kind of rebellion, followed by distancing. Instead of recognising this as the time for *rapprochement*, the urge is to withdraw, usually permanently.

The search for self, for passion, becomes the focus in the quest for happiness, and the effort needed to save a marriage seems lacklustre by comparison.

And so, divorce and remarriage become the solution, bringing further complexities in their wake, especially if there are children to consider. It is difficult enough to be a married parent, even more difficult to be a single parent or a remarried parent, or of course a stepparent.

Given the situation, the need for widespread counselling and conciliation services for divorce is enormous and urgent. Ex-couples who become single parents and remarried parents need to find ways to reduce friction and regain at least a positive working relationship with each other, for their own sakes as well as the children's.

Remarriage needs to be seen as an opportunity to create a new kind of extended family which can welcome the absent biological parent and grandparents too, and which can acknowledge roots and widen networks without threatening the central couple in their loyalty to each other.

Human beings are adaptable. They can turn disadvantage to advantage. Remarriage can be an example of generosity and cooperation, of loving and trusting, and of forgiveness and large mindedness. If it is to provide human happiness, that's how it has to be.

STATISTICS

1 in 10 marriages ends in divorce by the sixth anniversary; 1 in 5 by the twelfth anniversary. Overall, 1 in 3 marriages will end in divorce if present trends continue.

The average age for a man at first marriage is 26 years, for a woman it is 23.8 years.

The younger the wife at marriage, the greater the risk of divorce, irrespective of how long the marriage has lasted.

Unskilled manual workers and unemployed husbands are at highest risk of divorce.

Highest rate of divorce occurs 3 years after marriage, when one 1 in 30 divorces; the age group of the people involved is between 20 and 29.

About 10% of divorces are in marriages of 25 years' duration or more.

About 29% of children in divorce are under 5 years old.

1 out of 5 children can expect to see their parents divorce before their sixteenth birthday.

Between 25% and 30% of children lose contact with one parent very soon after separation.

1 in 3 marriages involves a remarriage for at least one partner.

About 1 in 6 marriages involves remarriage for both partners. Just over half of women aged under 35 at separation remarry within 6 years. Nearly a quarter remarry within 3 years.

About 80% of people divorcing under the age of 30 will remarry within 5 years.

A divorced woman who remarries is approximately twice as likely to divorce as a single woman who marries at the same age; a divorced man who remarries is one and a half times as likely to divorce as a single man who marries at the same age.

About 20% of divorces in 1983 involved one or both partners who had been divorced before; in 1976 the figure was 11.6% with a steady rise since.

(From Fact Sheet on Divorce and Remarriage, 1986, Family Policy Studies Centre and OPCS. Figures for England and Wales.)

BIBLIOGRAPHY

CHAPTER I

Marriage and Love in England, 1300–1840, Alan Macfarlane, Blackwell, 1986

For Better, For Worse, British Marriages, 1600 to the Present, John R. Gillis, Oxford University Press, 1985

The Beginning of the Rest of Your Life, Penny Mansfield and Jean Collard, Macmillan, 1987

Woman magazine, Evelyn Home column, 12.5.56; 30.4.66

A Woman's Place, Peter Wilsher, *The Sunday Times*, 2.5.82

The Business Amazons, Leah Hertz, Andre Deutsch, 1986

The Death of the Family, David Cooper, Penguin, 1971

Families and How to Survive Them, Robin Skynner and John Cleese, Methuen, 1984

What is to be done about the Family?, edited by Lynne Segal, Penguin, 1983

Ask the Family, National Council of Voluntary Organisations, 1984

Letter to *The Times*, 16.4.87

Marriage, Divorce and the Family, paper given by Dr Jack Dominian, U K Marriage Research Centre conference, 1981

CHAPTER 2

Vem ar det?, Family and Marriage, Encyclopaedia Britannica, page 163, 1978

Social Class and Socioeconomic Differentials in Divorce in England and Wales, John Haskey, Population Studies, 38, 1984

Teenage Marriage and Marital Breakdown: a longitudinal study, Kathleen Kiernan, Populations Studies, 40, 1986

Future Shock, Alvin Toffler, The Bodley Head, 1970
The Anatomy of Relationships, Michael Argyle and Monika Henderson, Penguin, 1985
Surviving the Break-up, Judith S. Wallerstein and Joan Berlin Kelly, Grant McIntyre, 1980
The Politics of Separation and Divorce: a study in Attitude Formation, Jenny Chapman Robinson, Department of Politics, University of Strathclyde
The Wasey Report, Wasey Campbell-Ewald, 1982
Marital Status and Well-being, Helen Weingarten, Journal of Marriage and the Family, August 1985
Grounds for Divorce in England and Wales, John Haskey, Journal of Biosocial Science, vol. 18, April 1986
Divorce: who gets the blame in 'no fault'? Marianne Takas, M S, February 1986
Divorce Matters, Martin Richards and Jacqueline Burgoyne, Pelican, 1986
Maintenance after Divorce, John Eekelaar and Mavis Maclean, Oxford University Press, 1986
Mixed Up with the Law, Alex Goldie, Marriage Guidance, winter 1985
Teenage Marriage and Marital Breakdown: a longitudinal study, Kathleen Kiernan
The Divorce Revolution, Lenore Weitzman, the Free Press, 1985
Children and Divorce, Economic Factors, Mavis Maclean and John Eekelaar, Social Sciences Research Centre for Socio-Legal Studies, 1983

CHAPTER 3

Future Shock, Alvin Toffler, The Bodley Head, 1970
Taking Another Chance on Love, Deborah Haber, *New York* magazine, 31.5.82
Remarriage of the Divorced in England and Wales, a contemporary phenomenon, John Haskey, Journal of Biosocial Science, 1983, 15, 253–271
Unpublished paper by Audrey Baker, at Remarriage study day run by the National Marriage Guidance Council, 5.6.86

Making a Go of It, Jacqueline Burgoyne and David Clark, Routledge and Kegan Paul, 1984

Divorce and Remarriage, a record linkage study, Richard Leete and Susan Anthony, Population Trends, 16, 1979

Divorce after the Act, Marriage Guidance, spring 1987

Perceived Causes of Marriage Breakdown and Conditions of Life, Ailsa Burns, Journal of Marriage and the Family, August 1984

A Second Chance of Love, Daily Mirror, 11.3.86

Second Wife, Second Best?, Glynnis Walker, Sheldon Press, 1984

Recycling the Family, Frank Furstenburg and Graham Spanier, Sage, 1984

How Important is Sex to a Happy Marriage? American Family Circle, 3.13.79

Marriage: research reveals ingredients of happiness, Daniel Goleman, *The New York Times*, 16.4.85

Patterns of Love charted in Studies, Daniel Goleman, *The New York Times*, 10.9.85

A First Counselling Session, Sasha Brooks, Marriage Guidance, winter 1985

Affective Self-Disclosure and Marital Adjustment, B. Davidson, J. Balswick, C. Halveso, Journal of Marriage and the Family, February 1983

Two Views of Marriage Explored: His and Hers, Daniel Goleman, *The New York Times*, 1.4.86

The Anatomy of Relationships, Michael Argyle and Monika Henderson, Penguin, 1985

CHAPTER 4

Remarriage as an Incomplete Institution, Andrew Cherlin, American Journal of Sociology, 86, 636–650, 1978

The Family Life Cycle, edited by Elizabeth Carter and Monica McGoldrick, Gardner Press, 1980

The Stepfamily Cycle, Patricia Papernow, Family Relations, July 1984

Stepchildren, Elsa Ferri, N F E R-Nelson, 1984

Problem Areas in Stepfamilies, Jo Ellen Theresa Pink and Karen Smith Wampler, Family Relations, July 1985

Children In The Middle, Ann Mitchell, Tavistock publications, 1985
Remarriage between divorced people with children from previous marriages, Lillian Messinger, Journal of Marriage and the Family, April 1976
Kids Compare Notes, M S, February 1985
Legal report, R v R, *Guardian*, 28.5.86
How Divorce Affects Teenagers, Helen Franks, *Good House-keeping*, August 1980
A Model for Stepfamily Development, David Mills, Family Relations, July 1984

CHAPTER 5

The Stepfamily Cycle, Patricia Papernow, Family Relations, July 1984
Making A Go Of It, Jacqueline Burgoyne and David Clark, Routledge and Kegan Paul, 1984
Divorce: who gets the blame in 'no fault'?, Marianne Takas, M S, February 1986

CHAPTER 6

Mitigating Anger in Divorce, report of talk by Judith Wallerstein, *The New York Times*, 6.5.85
Demographic Factors in the continuing relationship between former spouses, Bernard Bloom and Konnie Kindle, Family Relations, July 1985
Remarriage in Sweden, Jan Trost, Family Relations, July 1984
Quasi-kin relationships and marital quality in stepfather families, W. Glenn Clingempeel, Journal of Personality and Social Psychology, vol. 41, 1981
Preparation for Remarriage Following Divorce, Lillian Messinger, Kenneth Walker, Stanley Freeman, American Journal of Orthopsychiatry, 48 (2) April 1978
Second Wife, Second Best?, Glynnis Walker, Sheldon Press, 1984
The Family Life Cycle, edited by Elizabeth Carter and Monica McGoldrick, Gardner Press, 1980

CHAPTER 7

Making A Go Of It, Jacqueline Burgoyne and David Clark, Routledge and Kegan Paul, 1984
Incorporated Association of Preparatory Schools, annual conference 1979

CHAPTER 8

The Reconstituted Family, Estelle Duberman, Nelson Hall, 1975
Recycling the Family, Frank Furstenburg and Graham Spanier, Sage, 1984
The grandparent/grandchild relationship, Chrystal Ramirez Barranti, Family Relations, July 1985
Teenage Marriage and Marital Breakdown, Kathleen Kiernan, Populations Studies, 40, 1986

CHAPTER 9

Remarriage, Jessie Bernard, Dryden Press, 1956
Remarriage as an Incomplete Institution, Andrew Cherlin, American Journal of Sociology, 86, 636–650, 1978
Recycling the Family, Furstenburg and Spanier, Sage, 1984
The Risk of Dissolution in Remarriage, Frank Furstenburg and Graham Spanier, Family Relations, July 1984
Love's Labours Twice Lost, Lee Rodwell, *The Times* 14.3.86, quoting Dr Jack Dominian
Living Together, Clare Dyer, Marcel Berlins, Hamlyn, 1982
Quasi-kin relationships, structural complexity and marital quality in stepfamilies, W. Glenn Clingempeel and Eulalee Brand, Family Relations, July 1985
Common Problems of Stepparents and their spouses, Emily and John Visher, American Journal of Orthopsychiatry, 48 (2) 1978

CHAPTER 10

Divorce Matters, Martin Richards and Jacqueline Burgoyne, Pelican, 1986

A Family Approach to Conciliation in Separation and Divorce, Margaret Robinson and Lisa Parkinson, Journal of Family Therapy, 1985, 7, 357–377

Differences between conciliation and counselling, Thelma Fisher, Marriage Guidance, summer 1986

Relating to Marriage, papers from National Marriage Guidance Council study days on divorce and remarriage courses, 1985

Growing Up Divorced, Linda Bird Francke, Linden Press, 1983

Taking Steps, unpublished paper by Rachel Gilliatt and Gerv Leyden, from National Marriage Guidance Study day on remarriage, June 1986

Brief Marital Counselling with second marriages, Moyra Fryer, in *Relating to Marriage*, papers from National Marriage Guidance Council study days, 1984

Preparation for Remarriage following divorce, Lillian Messinger, Kenneth Walker, Stanley Freeman, American Journal of Orthopsychiatry, 48 (2) April 1978

INDEX

INDEX

Remarriage – *cont.*
religious wedding ceremonies, 43–4
role ambiguities, 102, 103, 130, 131–2
sex in, 58–9
social and economic facts, xi
social occasions, 144–8, 149
statistics, x, 1–2, 42, 46, 57, 153, 191
supportive, 117–19
see also Children; Stepfamilies
Richards, Martin, 34, 78–9, 166–7
Rob, 140–1, 157–9
Robin (Gill's son), 123–4
Robinson, Margaret, 154–5
Role ambiguities, 102, 103, 130, 131–2, 161
Role play, 174
Ronnie (50, taxi driver, Gill's 2nd husband), 18, 37–8, 123–4, 139, 147
Rosemary, 125–9, 130, 132, 144, 150–1
Rules, rule-making, 63, 81–2, 103–4, 159, 181
Ruth (Rob's 2nd wife), 141, 157–9

Sally, 106–7
Sam (Janet's partner), 70, 89, 113
Sandra (Steven's 2nd wife), 21, 22–3, 52, 88, 96–7
Scapegoats, 100, 108–9, 165
Self-disclosure, unequal, 61
Self-discovery, 4
Self-esteem, 10, 27, 32
Self-help, 176–83
Self-help society, 125–9, 151
Selfish genes, 141
Separation, 80
and children, 177–8
by mutual consent, (2 years), 14
handling of relationship in, 18–25
without consent (5 years), 14
see also Divorce
Sex, sexuality:
children's attitudes to adult, 69–71
go-slow techniques, 64
in marriage, 3–4, 15–17, 22–3, 24
pre-marital, 3, 4, 5, 69
and religious beliefs, 16–17
in remarriage, 58–9
Sexual incompatibility, 3, 15, 53
Sexual offences/abuse, 12, 84
Skynner, Robin, 6–7
Social occasions, 145–8, 149
private, 145
public, 145–8
Sociological parenting, xii, 73, 108
Spanier, Graham, 57, 58, 61, 89, 134, 160

Stepfamilies, ix, xii–xiii, 43, 65–83, 97, 129
children's response to stepparents, 71–4
contact with non-custodial parents, 77–9, 100, 101, 102, 134
courting couples, 69–71
discipline, 67, 68, 79–83, 96, 97
joint custody of children, 72, 77–8, 79
Papernow's seven stages of development, 66–8, 71, 81–2, 85, 86, 97, 188–9
preparation courses, 174
self-help, 179–81
sociological parenting, xii, 73
weekend visits of children, 74–7
see also Remarriage
Stepfamily Association, National, 66, 92, 93, 129, 163, 176
Sternberg, Dr Robert, 60
Steven (44, engineer), 21–2, 23, 52, 88, 96–7, 140
Straker, David, 172
Sue (49), 15, 46–7, 55, 119–23, 129, 130, 139, 150
Suicide, 20, 26, 40, 122
Supportive remarriage, 117–19
Surnames, problem of different, 73
Sylvia (mid-thirties, businesswoman, Bob's 2nd wife), 23, 51–2, 70, 87, 110

Takas, Marianne, 33, 91
Toffler, Alvin, 16, 42
Trial marriages, 16, 42

Unemployment, 34, 35, 36
'Unreasonable behaviour' as grounds for divorce, 14

Vaginal infection, 22–3
Violence in the family, 12
Voyeurism, 149–50

Walker, Glynnis, 105
Wallerstein, Judith, 26, 100
Wampler, Karen Smith, 68–9
Weddings, 2, 9, 147, 152
second, 1, 43
Weekend visits, 74–7
Weingarten, Helen, 27, 32
Weitzman, Professor Lenore, 35
'Wife sales', 9
Women's movement *see* Feminism
Workplace:
counselling in the, 170
nurseries, 171